Beachlife

Architecture and Interior Design
at the Seaside

Edited by
Clare Lowther and
Sarah Schultz

Frame Publishers,
Amsterdam

Beachlife~
Contents

Contents

04 Introduction

Leisure

- 08 Kupla, Ville Hara
- 12 Sea Baths Lourinhã, Carlos Mourão Pereira
- 14 Tungeneset Project, Code Arkitektur/Aurora Landskap
- 16 Floating Pool, Jonathan Kirschenfeld Associates
- 18 Skate Park, Acconci Studio
- 22 Ark-hive Concept, atomikarchitecture
- 24 Microcostas, Guallart Architects
- 26 National Tourist Routes, Rest Area, 70°N arkitektur
- 28 PS1: Loop, Höweler+Yoon
- 30 Kastrup Sea Bath, White Arkitekter
- 34 The Pulse, Andy Martin Associates
- 36 Bathing Beauties™, Michael Trainor/Atelier NU/i-am associates
- 42 Performing Arts Centre, Zaha Hadid/Patrik Schumacher
- 44 Strand aan de Maas, Monadnock
- 46 Lagoon Bathing Facility, Carlos Mourão Pereira
- 48 Lakeside Swimming Pool, The next ENTERprise
- 54 German Pavilion, Gruentuch Ernst Architects
- 56 Atomik Pier Concept, atomikarchitecture
- 58 Punta Pite, Teresa Moller Rivas
- 60 Mill, Sami Rintala/Janne Saario
- 62 White Sands Beach Pavilion, Wannemacher Russell Architects
- 64 PF1 New York, Work Architecture Company
- 66 Olympic Sculpture Park, Weiss/Manfredi

Hospitality

- 72 Aruba Bar and Restaurant, David Archer Architects
- 76 Hotel Kirkenes, Sami Rintala
- 78 The Library, Ms. Tirawan Songsawat
- 82 Hydropolis, 3deluxe
- 86 Chalet TOUCH, Nothing Studio
- 88 Indigo Patagonia Hotel, Sebastián Irarrazaval
- 92 Nestlé Bar, Fulguro
- 96 Fördehotel, Gruentuch Ernst Architects
- 98 Doen! Beach Club, John and Monique de Jong
- 102 Fifteen, Absolute Design
- 104 Sun Moon Lake Hotel, xrange
- 106 Supperclub, Concrete Architectural Associates
- 108 X2 Kui Buri, Duangrit Bunnag Architect
- 112 Zuri Bar, Gerd Couckhuyt/Modular Lighting Instruments
- 116 Floating and Rotating Tower, Waterstudio.NL
- 118 East Beach Café, Heatherwick Studio
- 120 Sixty Hotel, Studio 63 Architecture+Design
- 122 B2O, Concrete Architectural Associates

Art

- 126 Ghostnets, Virginia Reid/Jess Poulsen
- 128 Seapod, Louis de Cordier
- 130 Signpost 5, Florentijn Hofman
- 132 Ice Fish House, Satellietgroep
- 134 The world belongs to early risers, Barbara Visser
- 136 Hot with the Chance of a Late Storm, The Glue Society
- 138 Fles_en_Post, Satellietgroep
- 140 Wounded Falling Star, Rebecca Horn
- 142 Rubber Duck, Florentijn Hofman
- 144 Launch S.MAG, Satellietgroep
- 146 Bondi Beach/21 Beach Cells, Gregor Schneider
- 148 Tentstation, Melle Smets
- 150 Beach Animals (Strandbeesten), Theo Janssen
- 152 Festival of Light, Michael Trainor/Andy McKeown
- 154 Nomade, Jaume Plensa
- 156 Alluvial Sponge Comb, Anderson Anderson Architecture
- 158 Mussel Chair, Zeger Reyers
- 160 More/Less, Ellie Nuss/James McDermid
- 162 Skywalkers, FriendsWithYou

Residential

- 168 Villa Soravia, Coop Himmelb(l)au
- 172 Floating House Chatou, Ronan and Erwan Bouroullec
- 174 Beach House Malibu, Michael Maltzan Architecture
- 176 Poli House, Pezo von Ellrichshausen Architects
- 180 Writers Block I, Cheng+Snyder
- 182 The Distributed House, Office for Metropolitan Architecture
- 186 Casa de Alcanar, Carlos Ferrater/Carlos Escura
- 190 Single Hauz Concept, Front Architects
- 192 Private Residence, Lazzarini Pickering Architetti
- 196 Marina, Rojkind Arquitectos
- 198 Floating House, MOS
- 202 O House, Philippe Stuebi Architekten
- 206 Landmark Houses, Will Alsop/Sarah Featherstone/Piers Gough
- 210 Housing Block, Ofis Arhitekti
- 212 Light*house, UNStudio/3XN/Gehl Architects
- 214 Periscope Houses, Joke Vos architecten
- 218 Floating Home, Gruentuch Ernst Architects
- 220 Flooded Future 2050, Anthony Lau
- 226 Seaside Apartment, Doorzon Interior Architects
- 230 Floating House Concept, Markus Wikar
- 232 Living in Nature, IUAV students
- 236 Stilt Houses, Waterstudio.NL
- 238 Las Arenas Beach House, Javier Artadi

Products

- 242 SunShade, Lianne van Genugten
- 243 Cube, Jan Melis
- 244 Canasta, Patricia Urquiola
- 245 Bok.shovelseat, Sander Bokkinga
- 246 Step, GAEAforms
- 248 Quicnic, Students of the HfG-Karlsruhe
- 249 Bronco, Corral, C'upsidedown, Extremis
- 250 Umbella, The Nomad Concept/L' Anverre
- 251 Dream of Sand, Nacho Carbonell Ivars
- 252 B'kini Chair, Wiel Arets
- 253 Matryoshka Chair, Danny Fang
- 254 Chairbag, PS Lab
- 255 OneQ, Jan Willem Marijnissen
- 256 Chubby, Marcel Wanders
- 258 Basic+, Benedikt Aschatz
- 259 Leaf Hammock, GAEAforms
- 260 Schwimmfluegelhocker, David Olschewski
- 261 Pewter Stool, Max Lamb
- 262 Walden, Nils Holger Moormann
- 264 Loop Chairs, Höweler+Yoon Architecture
- 265 Al Fresco, José A.Gandia
- 266 By the Pool, Arne Quinze
- 267 SouthBeach, Christophe Pillet
- 268 The Swiss Benches, Alfredo Häberli
- 269 Mare, Verónica Martínez
- 270 Diversity, Herman Lijmbach
- 271 On the Ground, Livia Lauber
- 272 Somertroon, Gisele Somer
- 274 Fat Knit Hammock, Bless
- 275 Pharao, Alfred van Elk
- 276 Pachific.minimal lounge, fries&zumbühl
- 277 IZ, Francesc Rifé

279 Colophon

Beachlife~
Contents

Introduction~

Text by Satellietgroep

The sea belongs to everyone and thus to no one—words that not only define the world's largest public space but also leave it unarticulated. Oceans, seas and coastal regions are under tremendous pressure, worldwide. Faced with the prospect of global warming, economic and functional interests are competing for space. The changes anticipated are not only gargantuan but also geographically, ecologically, conceptually and philosophically unique. Shifting circumstances raise questions about new land, new (coastal) landscapes, new forms of urbanization and new offshore projects of various types. But the sea has a cultural significance as well. Its infinite space, timeless aura, tidal currents and empty horizon appeal to universal feelings of freedom and adventure. As our oceans stand on the threshold of great change, opportunities are emerging for new uses, different meanings and unprecedented approaches. This is the moment for a qualitative stimulus based on the development of specific characteristics of the sea from a cultural perspective. Artists, designers, architects and scientists are at the forefront of a different kind of thinking about—and a new way of experiencing—the qualities and problems of the sea. From nature to culture... and from concept to materiality.

Climate change and the encroaching seas have made aquatic living a topical subject in all parts of the globe. Architect Anthony Lau has responded to the climate changes with a proposal for floating communities that use decommissioned ships and recycled oil rigs as platforms for a new type of residential life on the water, a project the architect envisions as reality by 2050. Lau favours the unique character of his residential typology over that of modular mass-produced housing. It may be far in the future before his plan is appreciated, but some architects have already taken steps to counter the threat posed by global warming. Anderson Anderson Architects, for example, has designed the Alluvial Sponge Comb—a water absorbing landscape element that can be implemented at the edge of the Mississippi River to control flood an erosion. Dutch firm Waterstudio.NL has designed Stilt Houses in IJburg—dwellings that promise to keep occupants high and dry even in the event of a flood.

For the time being, however, the shores of the mainland remain a popular spot 'on the water'. Vast vistas, unspoilt nature, and a sense of peace draw many to the coast—some who live there only during the summer and others who stay the year round. Certain seaside dwellings grab our attention because of their striking designs, such as The Distributed House, by OMA, on an island in the Bahamas. Each part of the residential complex has a distinct location, a situation that promotes the relationship between occupant and environment, as moving from one room to another requires an exploration of outdoor space that ranges from 'thick jungle' to 'the island's pink shores'.

People without holiday homes or permanent seaside residences can enjoy large-scale commercial and recreational functions on the world's beaches, such as seaside resorts, beach pavilions, waterside attractions and special events. Holiday-makers flock *en masse* to such touristic delights during the summer. A dining experience enhanced by a view of the water is possible thanks to an endless selection of seaside restaurants, cafés and picnic tables. Those looking for a bit more action can have great fun splashing in contemporary sea baths or practising their moves in coastal skate parks. When there is no seaside nearby, the urban beaches are a welcome alternative. Riversides are covered with sand, well designed—often temporary—beach clubs are installed, and the city is ready for the sun to come out.

Works of art play an important role in today's seaside experience as well. Art is often able to express the spatial and social qualities—as well as the problems—of our coastal areas, and to make them surprisingly accessible to the public. An example is the melting ice-cream van that The Glue Society exhibited at Australia's Sculpture by the Sea Festival in an attempt to draw attention to global warming. Less amusing is the work of photographer Barbara Visser, whose photographic collection of posters, The world belongs to early risers, gives an entirely different twist to a day at the beach. It's works of art such as these that transform a destination normally marked by consumption and recreation into a platform for serious communication.

The diversity of coast and sea—and everything involved in that diversity—is fully covered in Beachlife. Here you will find a broad selection of art; architecture; and interior, landscape and product design; from exciting projects already completed to high-profile proposals for the future. The aim of the book is to inspire readers and to raise interest in the continued creation of quality seaside projects throughout the world.

Satellietgroep~

Satellietgroep is an artists' initiative created in 2006 in The Hague, The Netherlands, for the purpose of studying the cultural significance of oceans and seas from the perspective of the arts and science. The group's founders are Jacqueline Heerema (visual artist), Marianne Volleberg (anthropologist), Andries Micke (architect), Bas de Koning and Hederik van der Kolk (the graphic designers of creative collective Duel), and adviser Denis Oudendijk (architect). They challenge artists, designers, (landscape) architects and scientists to develop new concepts and projects that articulate a cultural, innovative and sustainable significance of the sea and her coasts.
Satellietgroep's projects include Satellieteiland, Zeedelijk, S.MAG (Sea Magazine) and EXOOT, all of which are aimed at securing a position for art and culture on seas and in coastal areas across the globe.

www.satellietgroep.nl

Beachlife~
Leisure

Leisure

Architect~
Ville Hara/
HUT wood studio

Client~
Korkeasaari Zoo

Lighting consultant~
Insinööritoimisto Olof Granlund Oy

Structural engineer~
Nuvo Engineering

Manufacturers~
Finnforest Kunigaspalkki, Elixi, MiTek, SFS-Intec

Total surface (m²)~
82

Completed~
2002

Website~
www.avan.to

Photography by
Jussi Tiainen,
HUT/A photo lab

Beachlife~
Leisure

The winning entry of a competition organized by Helsinki's Korkeasaari Zoo, in collaboration with Wood Focus Finland, Kupla (Finnish for 'bubble') is a 10-m-high viewing tower which stands like an architectural nest 18 m above sea level on the rocky island of Korkeasaari. After the laborious task of building a 2-m-high, 1:5 scale model of his design and initiating full-scale test battens to monitor the structure's tolerance, architect Ville Hara—together with a team of eight international architecture students—constructed his design on site. The delicate form is based on that of an eggshell; the structure remains stable even though its latticework envelope, which is held together by more than 600 bolted joints, is punctured by a large ground-level entranceway. Made from 72 battens, twisted and bent to display no fewer than seven preformed curves, the two-storey structure—open on all sides—encloses visitors while also exposing them to views of the sea and the zoo. Stairs zigzag to the top, where an oval 'skylight' permits an unobstructed view of the heavens. Applied as weatherproofing, a substance containing linseed oil was used to treat the timber. Hara, who often draws inspiration from nature, favours curvilinear shapes—which he relates to the human physique—over rectilinear forms, and we expect visitors to the Korkeasaari Zoo would agree.

01~
Having weathered to a silvery grey, the timber tower blends beautifully into the scenery.

02~
Architect Ville Hara drew inspiration for the tower's delicate organic form from the site itself, which follows the surrounding stone wall and skirts a birch grove.

01

Kupla
Korkeasaari Island, Finland

03

04

03~
Visitors to the Korkeasaari Zoo, many of whom are children, approach Kupla as though it were a huge cage, allowing them to imagine being wild animals in the zoo. Others simply see it as a giant balloon made of wood.

04~
Stairs zigzagging to the top of the structure form Kupla's only enclosed space.

05~
Because Kupla stands on a rocky island 18 m above sea level, even though it's only 10 m high the tower provides a magnificent view of the surroundings, including city centre and seascape.

10 | 11

Beachlife~
Leisure

Project~
Kupla Korkeasaari Island, Finland

Architect~
Carlos Mourão Pereira

Collaborators~
Pedro Ferreira,
Luís Fonseca Rasteiro,
Ana Luísa Pedroso,
Daniel Oliveira Franco,
José Jorge Coelho,
Miguel Carvalho

Access consultant~
Jorge Falcato Simões

Marine-biology consultant~
Ricardo Melo

Landscape-design consultant~
Inês Campilho Chaves

Sustainable design consultant~
Manuel Correia Guedes

Structural engineer~
Miguel Villar

Hydraulic engineer~
Filipe Rêgo

Total surface (m²)~
464

Designed~
2007

Website~
www.carlosmouraopereira.com

Renderings by
Pedro Ferreira,
Luís Fonseca Rasteiro

Designed around existing structures dating from the mid-20th century, architect Carlos Mourão Pereira's bathing facility in Lourinhã, Portugal, has transformed redundant fisheries into outdoor baths. The result of a proposal to convert the old concrete structures into tanks containing sea water, the complex, situated on Paimogo Beach, features a large volume that accommodates smaller units. An outdoor fish tank you can swim in, Mourão Pereira's design also includes receptacles for various marine species, which offer human visitors a collage of textures and concavities to delight the senses.

Integrated within the rocky shoreline, the facility radiates an air of durability. The waves and tides of the Atlantic create a passive recycling system essential to the wellbeing of wildlife in the tanks. Ramps that trace the natural incline of the beach allow visitors to immerse themselves gradually in sea water baths with different water levels for swimmers and waders of all ages. For the visually impaired, information in Braille is found on handrails that surround the site. Set against a base of recycled concrete, the randomly shaped volumes of Mourão Pereira's design resemble miniature islands adrift in a mini ocean.

01—02~
Carlos Mourão Pereira's selected abandoned fisheries in Lourinhã, Portugal, as a location for his outdoors baths.

03~
Pereira's proposal, with a view of the main road to the beach.

01

02

Beachlife~
Leisure

Sea Baths
Lourinhã, Portugal

04~
Section showing the various depths of the sea baths and underwater vegetation.

05—06~
Proposed access point to the bathing facility and sandy beach.

03

04

05

06

Designers~
Code Arkitektur and
Aurora Landskap

Client~
The Norwegian Public Roads
Administration

Engineer~
B-consult

Manufacturer~
Senja Entrapenør

Total cost (£)~
370,000

Completed~
June 2007

Websites~
www.code.no
www.aurora-landskap.no

Photography by
Cato Lauritzen of
Lauritzen & Westh

Beachlife~
Leisure

Tungeneset Project
Senja, Norway

Inspired by an old Norse saying—'Whoever makes a journey has a story to tell'—the Norwegian Public Roads Administration is currently developing national tourist routes. Designed to showcase the country's magnificent scenery in a harmonious and non-exploitive way, 18 sections of the Norwegian motorway network are scheduled to become designated tourist routes by 2015. The first landmark attraction to open on the Senja route (Senja is an island in northern Norway) is the Tungeneset Project by Code Arkitektur and Aurora Landskap. This 80m long pathway to the sea is located at the tip of a peninsula between two fjords, providing views of the North Sea to the west and the Okshornan peaks to the north. Unwilling to cut into the landscape, Code Arkitektur and Aurora Landskap created a sturdy wooden trough that appears to skim over the surface of the terrain, zigzagging down to the seashore like an artificial stream. The path moves from a car park towards a barbecue area on the coastal rocks. The first 35m consists of a concrete ramp that traces the slope between the road and the picnic area. At the end of concrete stretch, visitors reach a small viewing point, which marks the safest place to stop when the weather is bad. Those who choose to continue their journey to the end of the jagged path can indulge in some waterfront dining. Forming a seamless integration between natural and artificial structures, a concrete section concludes the path. Selected for its neutral colour, the concrete blends smoothly into the rocky landscape.

01~
The wooden ramp leads to a concrete barbecue area by the sea.

02~
Walking towards a spectacular view of the North Sea and the Okshornan peaks.

03~
Concrete platform and wooden ramp.

01

02

03

Architect~
Jonathan Kirschenfeld Associates

Client~
The Neptune Foundation

Pool consultant~
Trace Architects

Engineer~
C.R. Cushing and Co.,
Robert Silman Associates

Manufacturer~
Bollinger Shipyard

Total surface (m²)~
2080

Total cost (US$)~
5 million

Completed~
June 2007

Website~
www.kirscharch.com

Photography by
Philippe Baumann and
Tim Schenck

Beachlife~
Leisure

Known as 'the floating pool lady', Ann Buttenwieser (director of The Neptune Foundation), has spent over 27 years campaigning to reintroduce the floating bathhouse—a popular attraction in the early 20th century—to the city of New York. Five million dollars later, Jonathan Kirschenfeld Associates entered the scene, and the dream became reality. Built for portability so that it can be docked in a different location each summer, the floating pool, an adapted steel deck barge, has a capacity of 175 people. To accommodate the hoards of visitors expected during the pool's inaugural season, a parking lot in front of the moored barge was transformed into an artificial beach. After basking on the sand-covered tarmac, guests could walk through the locker and shower rooms, past 12-m-long translucent aquatic-themed murals, and down a ramp along the edge of the barge to the pool deck. Seven lanes wide and 1.2 m deep, the 25-m-long pool turned an afternoon dip into a paradoxical experience. No matter how deep the swimmers went, they were always swimming above the water.

01~
The barge arrives in Brooklyn to be completed there.

02~
Sun court and spray pool.

03~
The pool deck against a background of the New York harbor.

01

Floating Pool New York, NY, USA

Skate Park
San Juan, Puerto Rico

Designer~
Acconci Studio

Client~
Department of Transportation and Public Works, San Juan, Puerto Rico

Consultant~
Zach Wormhoudt

Engineer~
Horacio Diaz & Associates

Total surface (m²)~
9150

Total cost ($)~
1 million

Website~
www.acconci.com

Renderings by
Acconci Studio

Beachlife~
Leisure

Riding the waves. A series of meandering tracks undulating up and down and in and out, Acconci Studio's concept for a new skate park in San Juan glides over the land and drops into the sea. Accommodating the existing features of the site, the skate park begins at the highest point of a ramp that crosses a pedestrian bridge. As the grassy track on either side of the walkway disappears, it is replaced by a strip of green concrete. Designed to echo the movements of a skateboarder, the strips roll down the ramps before waving up and swelling to consume as much space as possible. At the point where the two strips separate, one swerves to the hill, breaking into parts on its approach and curving around itself on impact to create a hole inside a hole—a proliferating sphere—while the other advances to the mound. Headed towards the ocean, looping and rising one step at a time, five paths on the slope turn and curve into quarter pipes, half pipes. Each has a different gradient. Amateurs practise on the shortest and shallowest ramp, while confident skaters are given free rein to challenge the longest and deepest. Budget permitting, Acconci will add a mobile ellipse to its original design: a kidney-shaped element featuring loops that react like a seesaw to skaters' movements. Picture a skater at one end of the ellipse, low to the ground, being suddenly lifted by the weight of a skater using the other end. Perfecting manoeuvres can be tricky when you're balancing on a piece of wood!

01~
At the bottom of the ramp, two skating strips rise and cross in midair over the walkway.

02~
Helicopter view of the skate park. Green gradually changes to blue, enhancing the visual flow from the grassy area to the sea.

03~
One skating strip loops around itself to create a skating platform below.

01

02

03

04~
Thanks to its varied heights, gradients and pipe lengths, the skate park has something for everyone, from inexperienced amateur to world-class skater.

05~
The edges of the skating strips are for grinding.

06~
One skating strip heads to the hill and breaks into segments that roll up and down towards the sea.

Beachlife~
Leisure

Project~
Skate Park
San Juan,
Puerto Rico

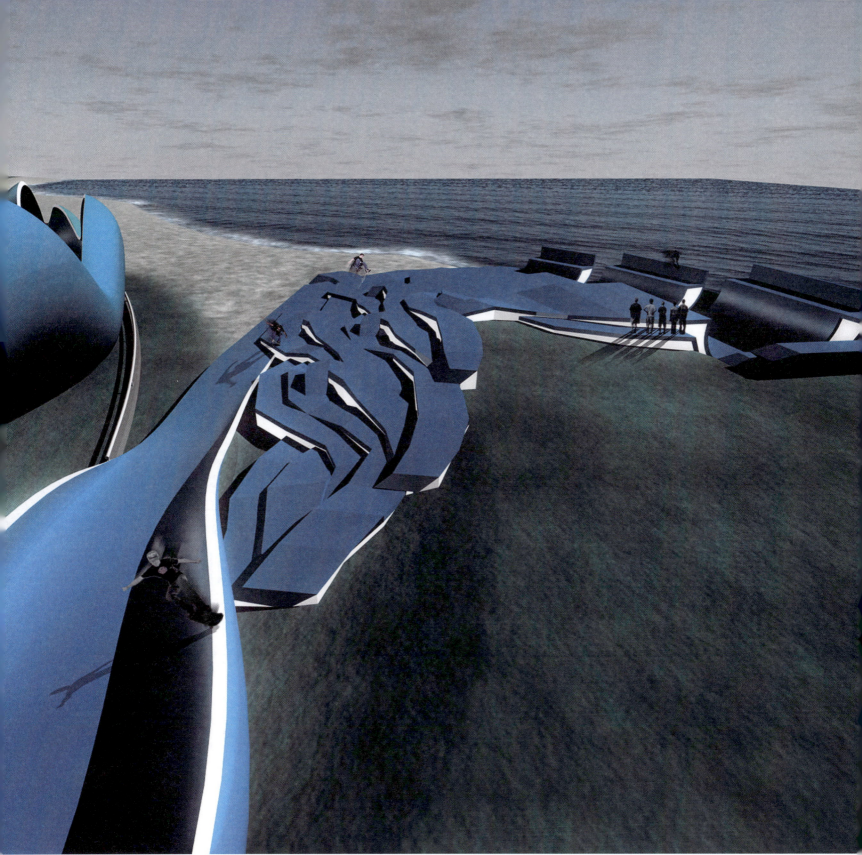

Architect~
atomikarchitecture

Client~
Bathing Beauties Competition

Model makers~
Simon Windebank, Lizz Riley

Designed~
2007

Website~
www.atomikarchitecture.com

Renderings by Mike Oades

Compared with treacherous seas and storm-strength winds, the threat of local vandals to atomikarchitecture's ark-hive is hardly cause for concern. Conceived in response to artist Michael Trainor's Bathing Beauties competition—for the design of a new range of 21st—century seaside shelters—atomik's shipping container-cum-beach hut draws inspiration from the human inclination to reuse found objects. It may seem an unusual choice—containers are rarely found among the pebbles and driftwood along the English coast—but atomik was prompted not only by the knowledge that often, after only one journey, containers are sold to be used for a variety of functions, but also by the structure's obvious connection to the sea. Ubiquitous and mysterious, the container resembles a modern—day treasure chest. With this in mind, the architects devised a cryptic access code of the type that accompanies every intriguing treasure trail. Visitors wishing to enter must first decipher a set of clues on the outside of the hut. Unlocked, the box reveals deckchairs, windbreaks, buckets and spades, as well as a stove and kettle. Several sliding panels can be employed as sunshades or seating. Arranged in different configurations, these panels create a personal space within any type of environment, from public building to remote beach. Forging a connection between the container and its surroundings is another unexpected treasure—a small library of local folk songs—which the architects suggest should be enjoyed between 'cups of hot chocolate and the ebb and flow of the tide'.

01—07~
Sliding panels in the shipping container—atomikarchitecture's ark-hive—invite users to discover all sorts of beach equipment and functional applications.

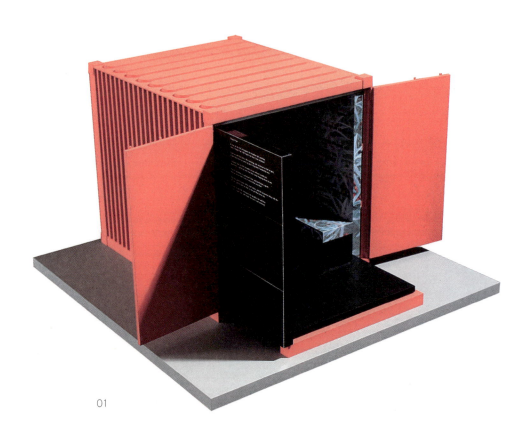

01

Beachlife~
Leisure

ark-hive Concept

02

03

04

05

06

07

Architects~
Guallart Architects,
Vincente Guallart,
Maria Diaz

Client~
Ayuntamiento de Vinaròs
Generalitat Valenciana
Ministerio de Turismo

Geometry consultant~
Marta Malé

Manufacturer~
Gestalt

Construction~
Binaria

Total length~
1 km

Total cost (€)~
600,000

Completed~
2006

Websites~
www.guallart.com
www.guallartblog.com

Photography by
Laura Cantarella,
Núria Díaz

Beachlife~
Leisure

Microcostas Vinaros, Spain

To transform a particularly rocky section of Spain's eastern shoreline into an accessible area for both tourists and residents, Guallart Architects created Microcostas, wood platforms that resemble clusters of limpets. Reflective of the asymmetry found in nature, the platforms—single units, but also grouped in smaller and larger arrangements—are dispersed along a 1-km beachfront site in various configurations. A geometric puzzle, Microcostas is based on a series of flat and peaked triangular frames designed to accommodate the uneven terrain. Surfaces on which to stand, sit or lie, the panelled decks provide a comfortable place to soak up the sun and admire the view.

Considerate of the existing landscape and conscious of the need to make a contribution that would enhance rather than decimate the coast of Vinaròs, Guallart commissioned Spanish firm Gestalt to build the platforms out of solid wood. 'We could do nothing less than add more quality material to a place already boasting extraordinary quality,' explains a Guallart representative.

01

02

03

05

01~
Hexagonal platforms arranged in a variety of configurations invite users to sit, stand, lean or lie down.

02—03~
Given a choice between the bare, rocky shoreline in this part of Spain and Guallart Architects' Microcostas, any sunbather would immediately opt for the smooth wooden surface of the latter.

04~
The shape of the Microcostas fits the rough terrain.

05~
Construction of the wood platforms on site.

04

Architect~
70°N arkitektur

Client~
Norwegian Public Roads Administration

Consulting engineer~
Norconsult

Manufacturer~
Mesta

Total surface (m²)~
190

Total cost (€)~
255,600

Completed~
August 2005

Website~
www.70n.no

Photography by
Vegar Moen,
Steinar Skaar

Beachlife~
Leisure

To experience the Norwegian countryside, the tourist does not necessarily have to leave his car. The Norwegian Public Roads Administration is currently implementing plans to transform 18 sections of the national roads into tourist attractions by the year 2015. Signs along the road point out rest areas, Kodak moments and parking facilities that invite the more adventurous types to leave their cars for a glacier hike or a mountain climb. At the Torvdalshalsen rest area, a 60-m-long wall provides shelter from the wind and, for visitors on the side facing the water, simultaneously blocks the car park from sight. Designed by 70°N arkitektur, the wall consists of a timber-clad steel frame displaying a horizontal linearity. Ramps and steps along the sunny south side of the wall offer visitors benches and tables. Low walls covered in darker boards radiate warmth when heated by the sun and double as backrests for the busloads of tourists who anticipate a comfortable stop with stunning views of mountains, fields and sea.

01~
The rest area, as viewed from the southwest, is accompanied by a car park, concealed behind an attractive wall that also functions as a wind screen.

02~
Following the contours of the site, the rest area features ramps and a wall designed to protect visitors from the wind.

03~
Integrated bench, table and screen ensemble.

01

National Tourist Routes, Rest Area Torvdalshalsen, Norway

02

03

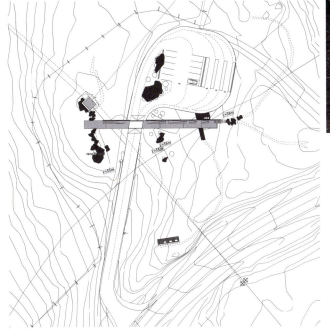
Site plan

Architect~
Höweler+Yoon Architecture

Clients~
P.S.1, MoMA

Structural engineer~
Markus Schulte

Total floor area (m²)~
1500

Total cost (US$)~
60,000

Designed~
2006

Website~
www.hyarchitecture.com

Photography by
Höweler+Yoon Architecture

An uninterrupted lattice of form outlining connections between spaces, Loop—part landscape, part infrastructure—is a jungle gym for adults and children, complete with pockets of interactive fun. Höweler+Yoon designed the concept for a competition organized by New York City's PS1 Museum of Contemporary Art. The brief asked for an installation to accompany the gallery's critically acclaimed summer music series, Warm Up. Resembling an urban beach, Höweler+Yoon's proposal features a porous structure equipped with motion sensors meant to set off waterfalls, foam chambers, bubble jets and the like: a range of responses triggered by human behaviour. Stretched horizontally and vertically, the cellular geometry of the structure consists of low surfaces for relaxing beneath a canopy that furnishes generous areas of shade and dramatic shadows. Outside the latticework, a bar area with an open dance floor serves as an outdoor lounge. Circulation routes at the centre of the installation keep the flow of traffic moving freely, whereas a more densely designed periphery encourages people to linger and mingle.

Loop aspires to be a completely immersive social environment: a compact landscape for the unpredictable unfolding of social exchange. By employing computational design and production techniques, and by combining interactive technologies with the right materials, Höweler+Yoon entered not only a competition but also a theoretical discourse devoted to the contemporary practice of architecture.

01~
Höweler+Yoon's model of PS1: Loop.

02~
Polypropylene was selected in part because it is nontoxic, nonflammable, easy to work with and completely recyclable.

03~
The lower latticework doubles as seating and lounge furniture, while the upper loops provide shade.

04~
Rendering of the shower area.

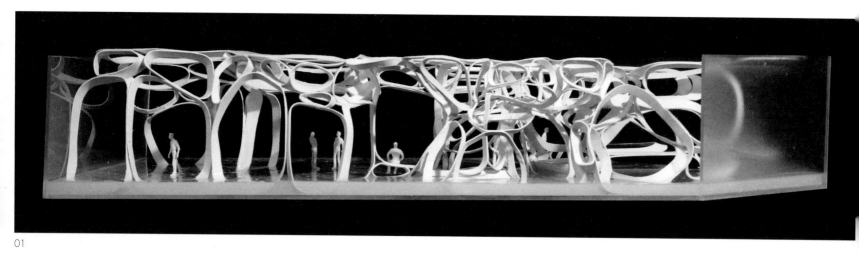

01

Beachlife~
Leisure

PS1: Loop
Long Island City, NY, USA

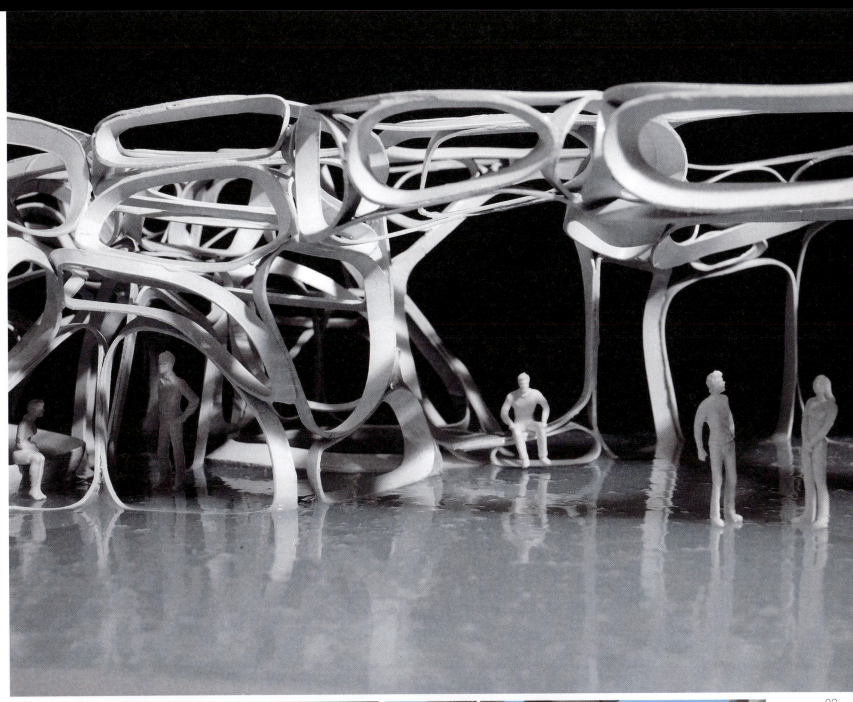
02

03

04

Architect~
White Arkitekter

Landscape design~
White Arkitekter

Client~
Tårnby Local Authority

Engineer~
NIRAS Rådgivende
Ingeniører og Planlæggere

Constructor~
Københavns
Dykkerentreprise

Completed~
2005

Website~
www.white.se

Photography by
Ole Haupt

Reaching into the Øresund from the Strandpark in Kastrup, White Arkitekter's Sea Bath forms an integral part of Kastrup's newly planned waterfront area. Built over the water, a wooden pier leads visitors from a service building on shore to the large circular construction at its far end, which gradually rises above the sea like a giant whirlpool to end in a 5-m-long diving platform. Perched on slender stilts and constructed from azobe, a wood selected for its durability in water, an 870-m² circular deck defines the interior space and provides shelter from the prevailing winds. Opening towards the shore, the structure invites visitors inside, while a continuous bench lining a section of the pier creates a rest and leisure area for those en route. In designing this untraditional framework for exercise and related activities, White Arkitekter presented the community with an environment that welcomes everyone, even those with physical or financial restrictions: admission is free, and ramps and other aids offer full access to less mobile visitors. Just call it 'a light at the end of the pier'. Emphasizing the sculptural form of the bath and allowing the complex to operate day and night, a series of uplights on the inner surface of the semicircular wall, together with two lines of LED spots along the pier, turn a dip in the Øresund into a dynamic experience. It's a project worth viewing: from land, sea or air.

01~
A wooden pier leading to White Arkitekter's Sea Bath provides a place for sunbathing and ends in a 5-m-long diving platform.

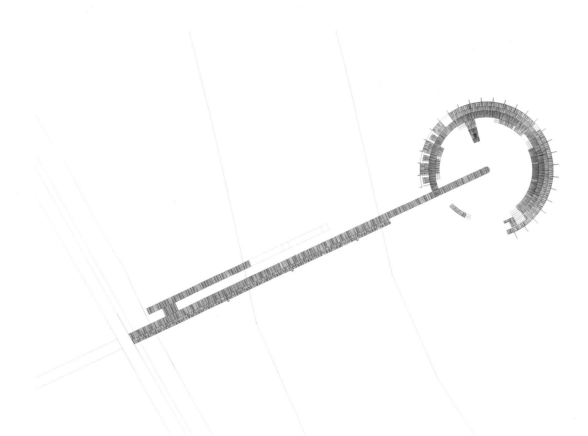

Beachlife~
Leisure

Kastrup Sea Bath
Kastrup, Denmark

02~
Sea Bath offers visitors 70 m² of changing facilities.

03~
Lighting design is the work of Erco.

04~
Slender stilts lift the Kastrup Sea Bath about 1 m above the surface of the Øresund.

02

03

04

Beachlife~
Leisure

Project~
Kastrup Sea Bath
Kastrup, Denmark

Architect~
Andy Martin Associates (AMA)

Client~
Another Department

Graphic designer~
Farrow Design

Engineers~
Arup

Project architect~
Simon Kwan Architects

Total surface (m²)~
22,660

Total cost (£)~
55 million

Duration of construction~
3 years

Completed~
September 2008

Website~
www.andymartinassociates.com

Renderings by
AMA

Beachlife~
Leisure

The Pulse Repulse Bay, Hong Kong

When the architects at Andy Martin Associates (AMA) refer to their new retail complex on Hong Kong's Repulse Bay as a pebble-based design, their description has nothing to do with the pebble-dash walls so popular in the 1920s. The Pulse, as AMA's shopping mall is called, is characterized by vast, pebble-shaped windows, a motif that continues in the form of decorative elements inside the complex. Dissected into organic blobs by a light-coloured band of fenestration—like a coastal line weaving around bays and beaches—the exterior of the volume merges harmoniously with its surroundings. A mixed-use development, lower in height than its neighbours and stretching half the length of the beach, The Pulse resembles a luxury cruiser marooned on land. Visitors to the 22,660-m² complex enter a fresh, relaxing interior that is synonymous with a resort environment. Intent on maintaining an 'outdoor connection' throughout the structure, AMA designed an area for alfresco dining on the upper level, where views of the sea accompany the cuisine, and, in the basement, fitting rooms and beach-related merchandise, another reference to the sandy shore just outside the door. Lush greenery enhances the courtyards of The Pulse, whose entrance welcomes shoppers with a 'sea' of sand and concrete.

01~
After a lazy day on the beach, one can enjoy alfresco dining on the rooftop terrace of Hong Kong mixed-use complex The Pulse, designed by Andy Martin Associates.

02~
The 250-m-long shopping mall runs half the length of the beach.

03~
The ground floor accommodates both retail and restaurants.

04~
Andy Martin Associates drew inspiration for the exterior of the complex from the organic forms of the many surrounding bays and beaches.

05~
A walkway under The Pulse provides direct access to the beach.

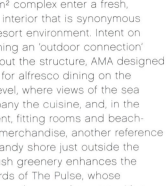

01

02

Bathing Beauties™ Lincolnshire Coast, UK

Competition~
Bathing Beauties™ 2006

Initiator~
Michael Trainor

Sponsors~
European Regional Development Fund, Lincolnshire County Council, East Lindsey District Council

Touring exhibition~
2008/2009

Come Up and See Me
Designer~
Michael Trainor

Materials~
Vitrified tiles, mirror, laminated plywood, galvanized steel

Halcyon Hut
Designer~
Atelier NU

Materials~
Cedar, acrylic resin

Jabba
Designer~
'i-am' associates

Materials~
Laminated plywood, paint, acrylic resin

Website~
www.bathingbeauties.org.uk

Photography by Michael Trainor, Quinlan Osborne

Beachlife~
Leisure

Initiated by artist Michael Trainor in early 2006, the international Bathing Beauties™ competition asked entrants to 're-imagine the beach hut for the 21st century'. The response was 240 scale-model entries from architects, designers and artists worldwide. All submissions could be viewed on the organization's website, but initially only five designs were selected for realization on the Lincolnshire coast. The organization eventually decided to commission at least three more to be built. Setting a good example, Trainor designed Come Up and See Me, a beach hut inspired by a popular cocktail: gin and tonic. The cylindrical hut integrates the notion of relaxation into a British sense of the surreal. Its shiny tiled exterior evokes the illusion of a highball glass, and a slice of lemon lights up the night. The top of the glass features a viewing platform with balustrade.

One of the original five winners of the competition was 'i-am' associates, a British design firm that submitted Jabba. In terms of concept, Jabba finds its origins in a primeval beach accommodation: the cave. Layers of materials such as glass, wood and aluminium were cut into shape with a waterjet before being assembled mechanically. Another winning design was the Halcyon Hut. Canadian architecture firm Atelier NU also revamped a traditional beach hut, but one less primitive than the cave. Constructed from red cedar wood and Plexiglas, the Halcyon Hut is a contemporary alternative to the popular pointed-roof beach huts found round the world. Other designs selected for realization were Eyes Wide sHut, A Hut for Gazing and Canoodling, and Oyster Pleasance.

01—03~
Come Up and See Me, by Michael Trainor, resembles a giant gin and tonic. A staircase spirals around the inner wall all the way to a platform on the roof where the drinking straws are actually hollow tubes that channel sunlight into the beach hut.

01

02

04~
The Halcyon Hut is a contemporary version of the popular pointed-roof beach hut.

05~
The front and back walls of the Halcyon Hut feature large pivoted doors that allow users to open the structure from both sides.

06 & 08~
At night, light inside the Halcyon Hut penetrates Plexiglas strips to create a random pattern of stripes glowing in the dark.

07~
Interior view of Atelier NU's Halcyon Hut.

04

38 | 39

Beachlife~
Leisure

Project~
Bathing Beauties™
Lincolnshire Coast, UK

05

06

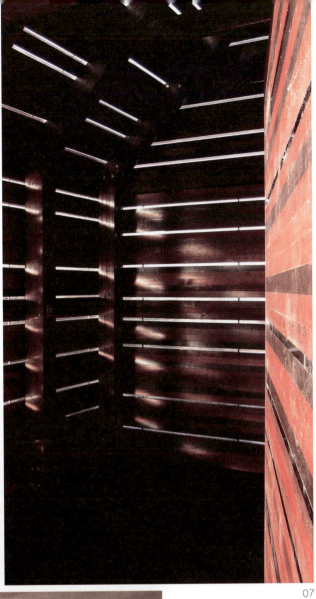

07

08

09~
Walking up the ramp, through the sliding doors and into Jabba, you find yourself immersed in the aroma of cedar wood tinged with a salty sea breeze.

10~
The various materials used for 'i-am' associates' Jabba beach hut have different weathering processes, which should prove interesting as the structure ages.

Beachlife~
Leisure

Project~
Bathing Beauties™
Lincolnshire Coast, UK

Architects~
Zaha Hadid,
Patrik Schumacher

Client~
The Tourism Development
and Investment Company
of Abu Dhabi

Consultants~
Anne Minors
Performance Consultants,
Sound Space Design,
WSP Group

Total surface (m²)~
62,770

Completed~
To be completed

Website~
www.zaha-hadid.com

Renderings by
Zaha Hadid Architects

1~ Foyer
2~ Recital hall
3~ Opera house
4~ Playhouse theatre
5~ Fine-dining restaurant
6~ Café
7~ Terrace
8~ Retail
9~ Press-conference area
10~ Parking

With a slither and a nearly audible sigh, Zaha Hadid and Patrik Schumacher's serpentine Performing Arts Centre in Abu Dhabi creeps from the city on its way to the sea, apparently in search of water. The reptilian complex resembles a growing multi-layered organism sprouting a network of successive branches. Hadid has said that 'as it winds through the site, the architecture increases in complexity, building up height and depth and achieving multiple summits in the bodies housing the performance spaces, which spring from the structure like fruits on a vine to face the water in the west'. The building, which reaches a height of 62 m, becomes, she says, 'part of an inclining ensemble of structures that stretch from the Maritime Museum at its southern end to the Guggenheim Abu Dhabi at the northern tip. With its centre of mass at the water's edge, the Performing Arts Centre focuses its volume along the central axis of the site. This interrupts the block matrix at the Arterial Road, opening views to the sea and the skyline of Abu Dhabi.' Also designed for optimum views is the wide, shaded roof terrace of the restaurant, where alfresco dining offers guests direct contact with the great outdoors. Huge windows in the concert hall (positioned above a quartet of theatres) serve as a pertinent reminder of the site's seafront orientation. Out of the sun, situated in the eastern tail of the serpent, retail areas attract those using the footbridge that links the Performing Arts Centre to the central pedestrian zone—perfect for the purchase of a new leotard before rehearsal!

01~
A pedestrian corridor connects the Sheikh Zayed National Museum to the seafront promenade in Abu Dhabi.

02~
Birds-eye view of the Performing Arts Centre from the east. The complex was designed by Zaha Hadid and Patrik Schumacher.

01

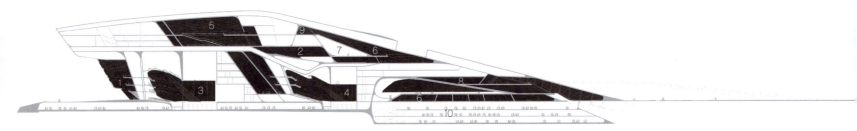

Beachlife~
Leisure

Performing Arts Centre Abu Dhabi, United Arab Emirates

03~
Birds-eye view of Abu Dhabi's new Performing Arts Centre from the northwest.

04~
The main concert hall is located above four other theatres. Huge windows behind the stage allow daylight to enter the hall, while also offering great views of the city skyline and the sea.

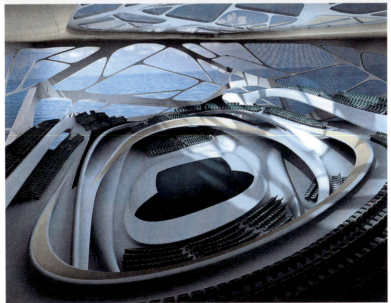

Architect~
Monadnock

Client~
Stichting Strand aan de Maas

Manufacturer~
K&A Group

Completed~
May 2007

Website~
www.monadnock.nl

Photography by Jeroen Musch

In the summer of 2007, a large red façade blatantly bearing the word strand announced a temporary urban beach in Rotterdam: a treat for visitors to one modest section of the city's overwhelming riverside port. The project, called Strand aan de Maas (Beach on the Maas), had two distinct faces. The Strand aan de Maas pavilion, designed by Monadnock, harmonized with its urban surroundings at the front while forming the perfect foil for beach activities at the back. Lying on layers of glistening sand was a welcome alternative to sunbathing on a strip of pavement, and the two-tiered pavilion—constructed in just three weeks—featured overhanging verandas, which sheltered visitors from the midday sun, an outdoor bar and a kitchen, where snacks were prepared. Steps built into the existing structure of the harbour led directly to the balcony of the pavilion, where guests had magnificent views of the waterfront, the urban skyline and those toasting in the sun one level below. Part of Rotterdam's 2007 City of Architecture festival, an initiative organized to celebrate the city's architectural culture, Monadnock's temporary pavilion attracted a bevy of tourists and locals—especially when the sun was shining.

01~
In the summer of 2007, stairs led visitors to the entrance building of an urban beach in Rotterdam.

02~
The closed structure was a prominent element within its urban surroundings.

03~
Beach side. The terrace offered a view of the River Maas.

04~
View through the staircase.

01

Beachlife~
Leisure

Strand aan de Maas Rotterdam, the Netherlands

02

03

04

Lagoon Bathing Facility
Grândola, Portugal

Architect~
Carlos Mourão Pereira

Client~
Câmara Municipal de Grândola

Collaborators~
Duarte Ramos,
Ana Luísa Pedroso,
José Jorge Coelho,
Luís Fonseca Rasteiro,
Mónica Coutinho,
Raquel Matela

Access consultant~
Jorge Falcato Simões

Marine-biology consultant~
Ricardo Melo

Landscape-design consultant~
Carlos Alves

Sustainable design consultant~
Manuel Correia Guedes

Structural engineer~
Miguel Villar

Hydraulic engineer~
Filipe Rêgo

Designed~
2008

Website~
www.carlosmouraopereira.com

Renderings by
Duarte Ramos

Beachlife~
Leisure

Proposed for Portugal's Melides Lagoon, Carlos Mourão Pereira's bathing facility seeks to create an inclusive bathing structure with a thematic garden reflective of the botanical content of its aquatic setting. Pereira's facility—a structure aimed at rehabilitating the ecosystem of a lagoon known for the poor quality of its water—would establish a safe site for children, away from the crashing waves and strong currents that characterize this stretch of the Atlantic coast. Extending from the beach like a sunken pier, the bath, which rests on a base of translucent recycled concrete, features a main tank that is divided into a number of areas. Curving up and breaking the surface of the water, like fish gasping for air, the tips of underwater loungers signal places of relaxation. A sensorial experience that encourages visitors to tune into birdsong and the sounds of the sea, while enjoying the scent of Melides' cane plantation, the bath includes marine life contained in smaller units throughout the site. Foreseen as an environment that will become self-sufficient in time, the project is based on the use of water from an existing spring, which is to be gradually replaced by decontaminated water from the lagoon.

01~
The main tank of Carlos Mourão Pereira's proposal for Grândola, Portugal, has more than a recreational function; it would also help to rehabilitate the local ecosystem.

02~
View from the main road of the proposed bathing facility, which extends inland from the Melides Lagoon. Water in the lagoon is not yet clean enough for swimming. Other problems include strong currents and species of marine life bordering on extinction.

03~
Underwater loungers in the tanks provide a place for relaxation.

04~
Entrance point to the proposed bathing facility.

01

02

03

04

Architect~
The next ENTERprise

Client~
Comune di Caldaro

Project manager~
Studio comClic

Structural engineer~
Bergmeister & Partner

Structural concept~
Bollinger+Grohmann

Partner office~
Plan Werk Stadt,
Dellago Architekten

Lighting design~
Ploderer & Partner

Landscaping~
Land in Sicht

Total area (m²)~
10,800

Completed~
May 2006

Website:
www.thenextenterprise.at

Photography by
Lukas Schaller,
the next ENTERprise

Beachlife~
Leisure

Cultivating the only public bathing site on Italy's Lake Caldaro—a nature reserve on the northern shore—the next ENTERprise realized a venue for culture and community life, where public space and protected areas merge to form a continuous terrain. Perched on an existing slope, the swimming pool is organized on two levels to maximize floor space. On the upper level, a public sun deck extending towards the lake borders the swimming area. An aquarium beneath this deck—it'defined by the varying depth of the pool—shelters guests from sunshine and rain. The round openings in the ceiling that visually connect the underground space to the upper level, offer a rippled view of bikini-clad bodies backed by the azzurro of a bright Italian sky. Suggestive of the movement below, two light shafts break through the surfaces of sun deck and swimming pool, emerging from the water like artificial rock formations. Back on dry land, steps connecting the deck and lower-level aquarium provide platforms for sunbathing and tiered seating for events hosted at the lake. Another angular form, appearing to float above the deck, is a canopy over the bar, which creates a covered eating area.

01~
Panoramic view of the sun deck and Lake Caldaro.

01

Lakeside Swimming Pool Caldaro, Italy

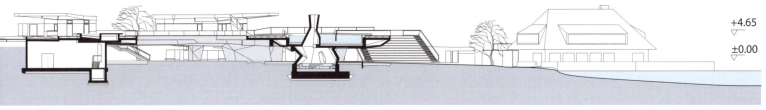

Longitudinal section

02~
A view of the aquarium space looking west, including tiered seating (left).

03~
Light visible through openings in the bottom of the pool illuminates the floor of the aquarium. The entrance to the whirlpool, housed in a hollow structural element, can be seen at the centre of the picture.

04~
Inside the Rainroom.

02

03

Beachlife~
Leisure

Project~
Lakeside Swimming Pool
Caldaro, Italy

1~ Promenade
2~ Tickets/first aid/ attendants
3~ Sun deck
4~ Access to sunbathing area
5~ Sunbathing area
6~ Playground
7~ Children's pool
8~ Atrium
9~ Shop/lavatories/bar
10~ Swimming pool
11~ Rainroom core
12~ Rainroom
13~ Whirlpool core
14~ Whirlpool
15~ Aquarium
16~ Lockers/showers
17~ Glow room
18~ Bleachers
19~ Kitchen
20~ Access to restaurant
21~ Restaurant
22~ Technical equipment
23~ Storage

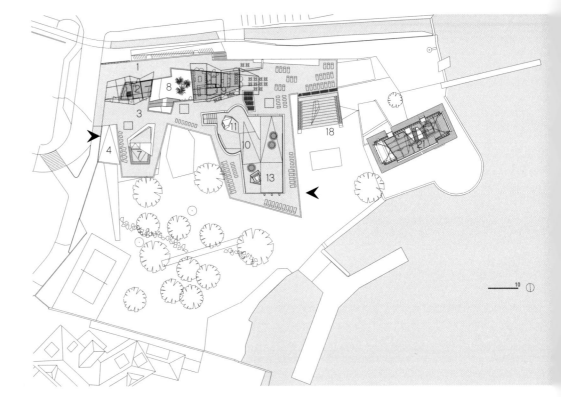

Ground level

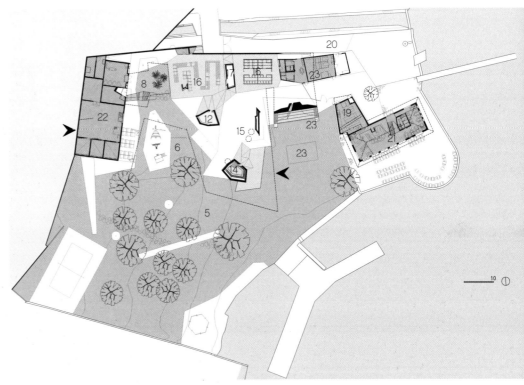

Lower level

Beachlife~
Leisure

Project~
Lakeside Swimming Pool
Caldaro, Italy

05~
The 'aquarium' space.

06~
View of the bath from the lake.

Architect~
Gruentuch Ernst Architects

Client~
German Ministry of Transport, Building and Urban Affairs

Event~
Venice Architecture Biennale

Completed~
September 2006

Website~
www.gruentuchernst.de

Photography by
Jan Bitter,
Gruentuch Ernst Architects

Beachlife~
Leisure

Bursting from the seams of the Giardini di Castello in Venice, the German pavilion with its rooftop terrace starred at the tenth Venice Architecture Biennale in 2006. The architects at Gruentuch Ernst created a structure that reflected the atmosphere found in Germany's big cities, where old and new converge with striking results. Added to the side of their design was a bright—red staircase, which jutted from the main hall into nearby greenery before continuing its ascent to the roof. The pavilion, which examined stimulating conversions of existing buildings and urban situations, not only served as a container for exhibits but also allowed guests to experience such metamorphoses first hand. Exposed, with a view that led the eye across tree tops towards the Adriatic Sea, the rooftop terrace surely turned the thoughts of visitors, at least momentarily, away from the architecture of the pavilion. Adding to the summery ambience, parasols and low white seating were scattered throughout the space, encouraging guests to linger.

01~
The rooftop terrace of the German Pavilion at the 2006 Venice Architecture Biennale offered visitors a view of cruise ships on the Adriatic Sea.

01

German Pavilion Venice, Italy

02~
Rendering of the pavilion by Gruentuch Ernst Architects.

03—05~
Visitors reached the rooftop terrace via a red staircase that started in a boxlike ground-floor volume and manoeuvred its way up, partly through the interior and partly around the outside of the building.

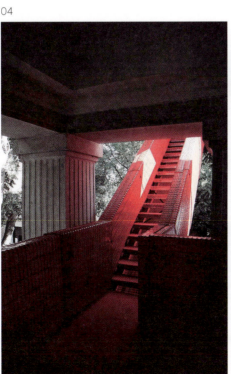

Architects~
Atomikarchitecture:
Christine Heil,
Mike Oades

Client~
BURA

Environmental
consultant~
XCO2

Designed~
2007

Illustrations by
Atomikarchitecture

Rendering by
Paul Madden

Winner of the professional category in BURA's 21st Century Pier competition, organized for the purpose of regenerating and renewing Britain's beach towns, Atomikarchitecture's Atomik Pier was designed as a centre of commercial and/or cultural activity. Recognizing that—despite their different geographical locations, demographics and industries—England's coastal resorts are united through social deprivation, high unemployment and an unbalanced ratio of young and old residents, the designers created a generic structure that can be adapted to any seaside location, regardless of local needs. Featuring an architectural knot that appears to anchor the structure to the shore, the Atomik Pier is based on a series of concentric rings arrayed around a central arena. Built to provide accommodation, the shell-like forms are orientated to maximize the use of the sun, while forming a shield against the prevailing winds. The architects foresee a number of possible scenarios for a complex envisioned as a pulse of social activity: a space for cultural events, an education centre, a site for extreme sports and a health spa, among others. These functions can be used as stand-alone concepts, but the designers suggest they be combined, 'in ways that two or three of the scenarios can coexist to provide a more sustainable social and environmental model'.

01~
One possibility is an Atomik Pier that includes a health spa.

02~
Another scenario is an Atomik Pier open at the centre to accommodate a marina.

03~
Atomik Pier consists of a series of concentric rings that encircle an arena, provide shelter from the wind, and maximize the warmth of the sun.

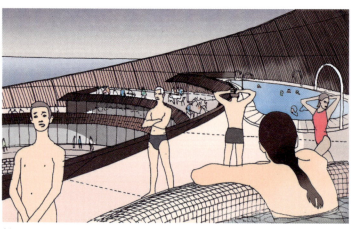

01

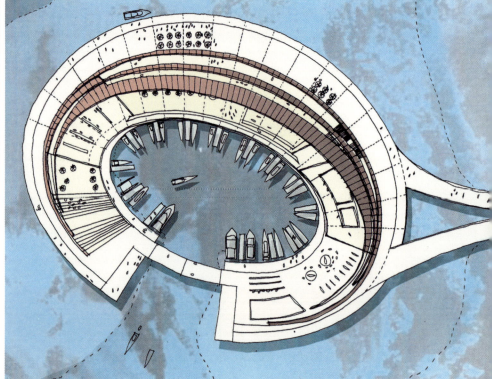

02

Atomik Pier Concept

Punta Pite
Zapallar to Papudo, Chile

Designer~ Teresa Moller Rivas

Client~ Conarq

Total length~ 1.5 km

Duration of construction~ 3 years

Website~ www.teresamoller.cl

Photography by Cristobal Palma

Connecting the dots, landscape architect Teresa Moller Rivas has created a trail along Chile's South Pacific coast that spans 27 acres and traces the contours of the bay between seaside towns Zapallar and Papudo. Twenty-nine spots highlighted along the way offer unique views of the ocean and indigenous vegetation. Scheduled to become a public path, the coastal trail is more death trap than sun snatcher, with steps positioned in the cliff face at such a steep vertical incline they all but disappear from the descending hiker's view. For those brave souls determined to survive unscathed, Rivas has included meeting places sculpted from the rocky cliff by Gerardo Aristia and small platforms on which hikers can gather. Despite its obvious allure to tourists, Punta Pite was designed to make future owners of the site aware of the natural, unspoilt beauty of the landscape crossed by the architect's treacherous trail.

01~ One of 29 designated spots along the Punta Pite trail that offer hikers scenic views of the Pacific.

02—03~ Punta Pite merges beautifully into its natural environment.

04~ Hikers can gather on platforms along the way.

05~ Narrow passages and steep flights of stairs turn the hike into an exciting adventure.

01

Site plan

02

Beachlife~
Leisure

Architects~
Sami Rintala, Janne Saario

Designed~
2007

Website~
www.samirintala.com

Renderings by
Sami Rintala

Designed as shelters for hikers or kayakers on Finnish rivers such as the Salo or Halikko, Sami Rintala's Mill is composed of elements that look like sections of a square tunnel, one midstream and the others poised on opposite sides of the river. The two angular volumes on the riverbanks—mirror images of each other—contain sleeping platforms and simple fireplaces. The self-sufficient wood-framed watermill in the water, between the two shelters, can generate enough electricity for lights and a radio. Intentionally light and open to heighten the visitor's sensory experience of the landscape, the structures are meant to be made from locally sourced wood. As selected sites are high enough to avoid problems linked to drift ice and flooding, Rintala's basic shelters can be inhabited whatever the weather.

01~
The name of the little ensemble is derived from the electricity-generating watermill between the two shelters.

02~
View from one of the shelters.

03~
Architect Sami Rintala designed the shelters for hikers and kayakers in Finland.

01

Beachlife~
Leisure

Mill
Salo, Finland

02

03

White Sands Beach Pavilion
Carrollwood, FL, USA

Architect~
Wannemacher Jensen Architects

Client~
Carrollwood Recreation District

Engineer~
Master Consulting Engineers

Construction~
Grosz and Stamper

Total floor area (m²)~
415

Total cost (US$)~
598,250

Completed~
June 2007

Website~
www.wjarc.com

Photography by James Borchuck

Beachlife~
Leisure

The two-part 'land and water' pavilion that Wannemacher Jensen Architects realized on Carrollwood's White Sands Beach (bordering a lake in central Florida) replaces a structure designed by Dean Rowe. The new pavilion, exposed to nature on nearly all sides, offers a brilliant view of beach, water and foliage, while creating a flowing transition from land to lake. The two volumes—positioned several metres apart but united in form—feature butterfly roofs that resemble a pair of gigantic seagulls gliding above the shore. A concrete walkway leading from the beached structure, which is anchored to the land by concrete and masonry, continues over the water as decking that serves as a stable platform for the second winged form. A skeletal version of the land pavilion, which includes a walled enclosure beneath the rear slope of its roof, the water pavilion is entirely open, and its roof rests on slender white columns. Echoing the deck below, panelled picnic tables invite visitors to indulge in some waterfront dining.
A platform for observation and recreation, the pavilion has a sensitive design whose simplicity provides a heightened experience of a pristine shoreline.

01~
Picnic tables beneath the roof of the pavilion provide a shady spot for lunch.

02—03~
The elongated pavilion blurs the transition between beach and water.

01

PF1 New York, NY, USA

Architect~
Work Architecture Company

Clients~
P.S.1, MoMA

Total cost (US$)~
70,000

Completed~
June 2008

Website~
www.work.ac

Photography by
Work Architecture Company

1~ Swings
2~ Night time column
3~ Soft column
4~ Mirror
5~ Farmer in picking hole
6~ Genie lift
7~ Graphics column
8~ Misting fans
9~ Herb tree
10~ Benches
11~ Butterfly bush
12~ The pool
13~ Pool seats
14~ Waterfall
15~ Periscope
16~ Clothes pegs
17~ Herb market
18~ LED sign

Beachlife~
Leisure

Winner of the Young Architects Program 2008, a competition organized by P.S.1 and MoMA, was Work Architecture Company, whose urban farm managed to occupy both courtyards—although the larger far more than the smaller—of contemporary art centre P.S.1. Accompanying Warm Up!, New York City's summer music series aimed at creating a multi-sensory experience for visitors, artists and musicians, PF1 (Public Farm One)—an architectural and urban manifesto designed to stimulate play and to reinvent the city—represented a new chapter in the ever-growing volume of leisure activities. Given a budget of $70,000 and asked to make a structure that included shade, water, seating and bar areas, Work Architecture built a structure out of hollow cardboard cylinders, fusing interior and exterior space within a colourful landscape. Ascending from a point more than 9m above the ground, the V-shaped garden gently sloped to the ground before curling to form a slight, asymmetric lip at the lower end. The installation, which promoted urban farming, included a wading pool—a nod to William Massie's Urban Beach (2002)—a farmers' market and the Kids' Grotto. Other noteworthy elements were the Grove and the Funderneath, a sensorial area with swings, tactile pillars and audio effects. Built from inexpensive yet sustainable materials and powered by solar energy, the installation was designed to be dismantled and recycled when no longer needed. Intended to bloom above the heads of visitors to Warm Up!, the botanical carpet resembled a miniature forest levered from its roots.

01~
Model of PF1 (Public Farm One) an installation by Work Architecture of New York City.

02~
The butterfly bush is located next to the pool.

03~
The entrance. Only the top of the garden is visible from the street.

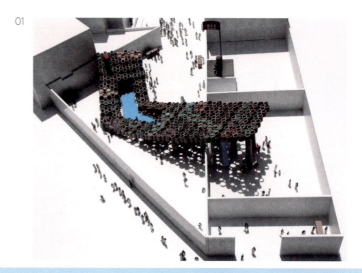

04~
View of the vegetable market and the periscope.

05~
The Funderneath area features swings.

04

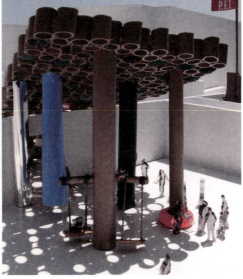

05

Olympic Sculpture Park
Seattle, WA, USA

Architect~
Weiss/Manfredi

Client~
Seattle Art Museum

Structural/civil engineer~
Magnusson Klemencic Associates

Geotechnical engineer~
Hart Crowser

Aquatic engineer~
Anchor Environmental

Duration of construction~
18 months

Completed~
January 2007

Website~
www.weissmanfredi.com

Photography by
Benjamin Benschneider,
Paul Warchol

Bisecting roads and railway lines in its quest for water, the Z-shaped Olympic Sculpture Park, one of the three exhibition sites of the Seattle Art Museum (SAM), zigzags down a nine-acre site to reconnect the city's urban core with the revitalized water—front of Eliott Bay. Responsible for the layered design is Weiss/Manfredi, a multidisciplinary practice whose 670m streak of green lightning, with its 12m change in grade, wanders from the city to the water's edge. Completed in 2007, six years after taking top honours in a competition that included entries from all over the world, the park features several permanent site-specific works that are carefully geared to the context. The slabs of Richard Serra's Wake rise from a ravine near the Gates Amphitheater, and as the angular path bridges the roadway and declines to the waterfront, it passes Mark Dion's Seattle Vivarium, Alexander Calder's emblematic Eagle and Tony Smith's Stinger. Visitors beginning their tour of the park at the exhibition pavilion and descending through the sculpture-enhanced gardens marvel as each stretch of Weiss/Manfredi's trail opens to reveal a different spectacle. The first section, which crosses the road, offers views of the Olympic Mountains; the second spans the train tracks and provides vistas of both city and port; and the last moves down to meet the water and a newly created beach. Deliberately open-ended, the design invites new interpretations of art, environmental engagement and the simple pleasures of life outdoors, while re-forging the fractured relationships of art, landscape and urban life.

01~
The pedestrian path leads to a promenade along Eliott Bay.

02~
Birds-eye view of the Olympic Sculpture Park.

Beachlife~
Leisure

01

03

04

03~
The Olympic Sculpture Park crosses both road and train tracks.

04~
Weiss/Manfredi moved art out of the museum and made the park part of Seattle's cityscape.

05~
One leg of the Z-shaped path spans the train tracks and offer a view of city and port.

06~
The trail creates a dynamic link of accessibility between the waterfront and the city.

05

Beachlife~
Hospitality

Hospitality

Aruba Bar and Restaurant Bournemouth, UK

Architect~
David Archer Architects

Client~
Andy Price

Project management~
PH Warr

Lighting designer~
Jonathon Coles

Construction~
Tekne Shop Fitting

Structural engineer~
Mann Williams

Service engineer~
Bourne

Furniture manufacturer~
Sitting Firm

Total floor area (m²)~
937

Total cost (£)~
1.7 million

Completed~
July 2007

Website~
www.davidarcherarchitects.com

Photography by
Keith Collie

Beachlife~
Hospitality

Inspired by Cinquante-Cinq in the south of France and Nikki Beach in Miami, the Aruba Bar and Restaurant—located in the middle of Bournemouth's seven-mile stretch of golden sand—offers Britain's beachgoers a cosmopolitan venue with 180-degree views across the whole of the bay. Positioned on the pier, an area alive with activity during the summer, the bar is one of a series of projects aimed at rejuvenating the UK's tired coastal resorts. A far cry from the stereotypic English seaside eatery, where chips are served in newspaper and tea is flavoured by more sand than sugar, Aruba offers a Polynesian, Caribbean and Pan-European menu and an extensive range of finely crafted cocktails. Directly accessible from the beach and open from 9 am to 2 am, Aruba is designed to attract tourists, business visitors, locals and second homers who spend their weekends at the beach trying to escape the London smog. A contemporary twist on a traditional beach hut, Aruba features pastel-painted tongue-and-groove interior walls and a 95-m² state-of-the-art island bar topped with polished zinc: the focal point of the 865-m² space. The bar and restaurant are furnished with bespoke banquettes, dining chairs, canteen tables and day beds. Despite a series of interventions—among which 4.5-m palm trees flanking the bar, sliding doors to the terrace, and outdoor showers promoting a relaxed drinking and dining atmosphere more commonly associated with resorts overseas—a mural of Poole Harbor, another of southern England's coastal tourist spots, reminds guests of the country they're in, even when the sun is shining!

01~
The terrace offers a view of Bournemouth's distinctive pier, which has the form of a circus tent.

02~
The bar, illuminated with wicker lanterns by Jonathan Coles, separates Aruba's dining, seating and lounge areas from one another.

01

Beachlife~
Hospitality

Project~
Aruba Bar and Restaurant
Bournemouth, UK

03~
The Aruba Bar can serve up to 40 people at one time.

04~
A fireplace enhances the cosy atmosphere.

05~
Diners arriving straight from the beach can avail themselves of the venue's outdoor showers before entering the restaurant.

06~
An image of Poole Harbour decorates the ceiling.

Architect~
Sami Rintala

Duration of construction~
10 days

Completed~
2005

Website~
www.samirintala.com

Photography by
Sami Rintala

Every second counts. Constructed in ten days and completed three minutes prior to its opening (with the help of three architecture students), Sami Rintala's Kirkenes Hotel provides rudimentary lodgings for passing fisherman. Situated on the coast of the Norwegian town of Kirkenes, the temporary accommodation was Rintala's response to a brief stipulating a site-specific work of art for a spot in the heart of town. The architect pushed the boundaries, however, and created a volume that is unequivocally functional. Flagged by a giant 'H' on one side of its black rectangular frame, the modest inn contains a single room, a double room and a lobby. Ironically, guests to the hotel—which may offer scenic views but is, in terms of size, very similar to a prison cell—are obliged to visit the police station next door for toilet and shower facilities. Rintala sees the structure as an alternative to the conventional hotel, which he says creates 'a evered reality'. Overlooking the Barents Sea, the hotel connects occupants to the great outdoors. As fresh as the winds whipping round its shell, the interior, paneled in white wood, bathes in a pool of light streaming through windows on the side facing the water. An economic design, the entire building is heated by a stove on the ground floor.

01~
Guests climb a steep ladder to reach the sleeping area.

02~
A stove covers the basic need for a heated facility. 'Unnecessary luxuries' such as toilet and shower have been eliminated to save space and money.

03~
The 'H' on the side of the temporary accommodation marks the small structure as a hotel.

04~
Front view of Hotel Kirkenes, which was designed by architect Sami Rintala.

01

02

Beachlife~
Hospitality

Hotel Kirkenes
Kirkenes, Norway

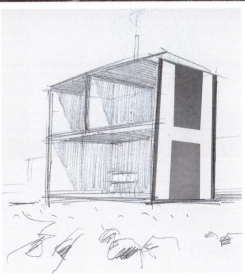

The Library Hotel
Ko Samui, Thailand

Designer~
Ms. Tirawan Songsawat

Client~
Design Hotels

Total surface (m²)~
6400

Total cost (£)~
370,000

Completed~
January 2007

Website~
www.designhotels.com/thelibrary

Photography by
Design Hotels

Situated next to the lively Chaweng Beach, a sandy stretch along the northeast coast of the Thai island of Ko Samui, The Library is a hotel designed by Ms. Tirawan Songsawat. The elegant minimalist structure is part of Design Hotels' chain of accommodations. Set in a lush landscape, the hotel offers visitors a total of 26 suites and studios spread over 6400 m² of beachfront property. Eager to preserve the site's natural ecology, Songsawat realized the design without the use of bulldozers. In addition to the ocean, certain rooms provide guests with a glimpse of age-old trees—lovingly preserved and now part of the complex—which reach to the skies. Interspersed with works of art, notably sculpture, the hotel and its surroundings boast a balance of nature and culture, in which verdant vegetation, blue water and pale beaches are offset by a bold colour scheme dominated by white, red, black and grey. Interiors bathed in an ultra-minimalist palette feature rooms whose furnishings descend in height to make the floor of each suite the centre of attraction: wall fittings are above beds that look down on sofas and, even lower, tables just centimetres from the floor. Exotic touches, such as adjustable wooden shutters, refer to the landscape right outside the door. Thanks to the designers belief that a good holiday equals an opportunity to enjoy a good book, guests are invited to be 'living sculptures' as they lounge on the terrace after selecting a title from the vast collection of books that gives the venue its distinctive name.

01~
At The Library on the Thai island of Ko Samui, a single row of sunbeds separates the swimming pool from the ocean.

02~
It's obvious how The Library got its name. Hotel guests arrive to find an extensive collection of books from which to choose.

01

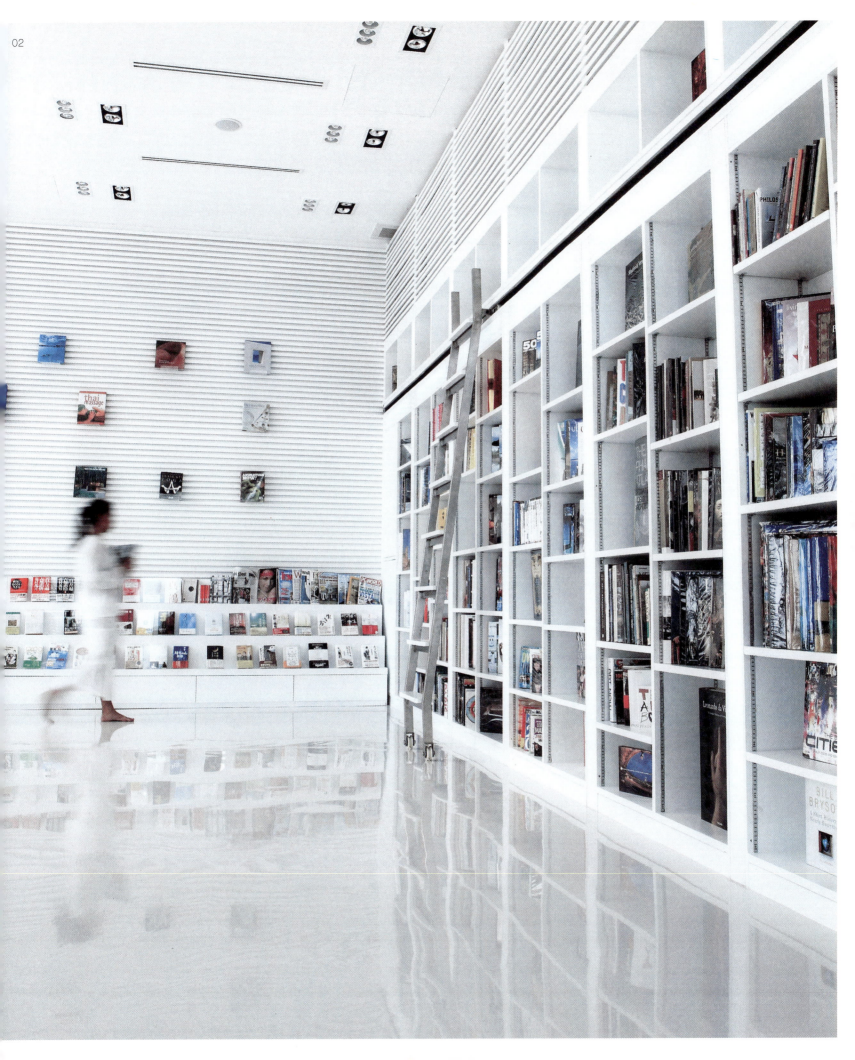

03

Beachlife~
Hospitality

Project~
The Library Hotel
Ko Samui, Thailand

04

03~
The hotel consists of 26 suites and studios in a lush landscape. During construction, bulldozer operators took the utmost care to preserve existing trees.

04~
Guests strolling through the hotel grounds find many white sculptures representing 'readers'. The figure shown here is enjoying a book on the restaurant terrace, which features an ocean view.

05~
A detail on the lawn at The Library.

06~
Architect Tirawan Songsawat opted for a palette of white, grey and red.

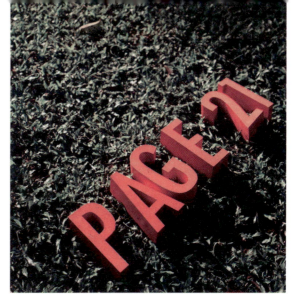
05

06

Designer~
3deluxe

Client~
Crescent Hydropolis Resorts PLC,
Joachim Hauser

Scheduled completion~
undisclosed

Website~
www.3deluxe.de

Renderings by
3deluxe

Although one Hydropolis complex is in planning stage in Dubai, for the most part this enticing concept by 3deluxe remains a series of architectural drawings representing underwater luxury hotels proposed for sites such as Oman, Qingdao and Monaco. Each holiday resort comprises a land station and hotel facilities, most of which are situated underwater. Emerging from the sea like computer-modified rock formations, the buildings, with their varying atmospheres and contemplative soundscapes, are described by the architects as having 'an intensive spatial impact that releases the visitor from ordinary perceptional structures and evokes complex sensual sensations'. Surrounded by a submarine waterscape, each hotel focuses on encouraging people to live peacefully alongside aquatic life. A connecting tunnel transports people by train from one area of the hotel to another. A more financially viable option than outer-space tourism, 3deluxe's underwater retreats offer even those who can't swim a chance to experience another world—a little universe that, if sea levels continue to rise, could duplicate the scene that many of us will see when we look out the window in years to come.

01~
Exclusive penthouses occupying the upper floors of the land station offer a fascinating view of the Hydropolis Hotel offshore.

02~
Rendering of the land station for Oman. A landing projecting into the sea corresponds to the form of the surrounding park, which creates traditional Arabic motifs around the land station.

03~
Land station with apartments, proposed for the Monte Carlo yacht harbour.

01

Beachlife~
Hospitality

Hydropolis Concept

03

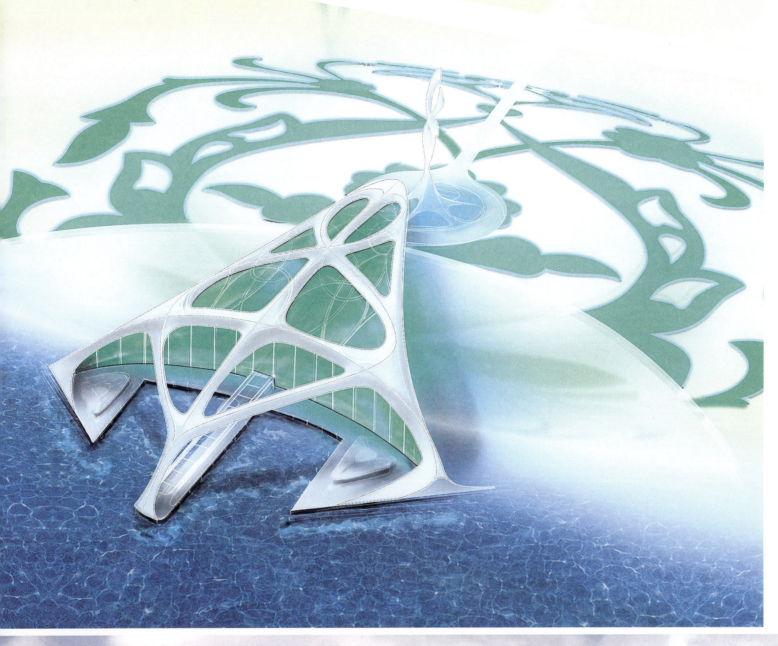

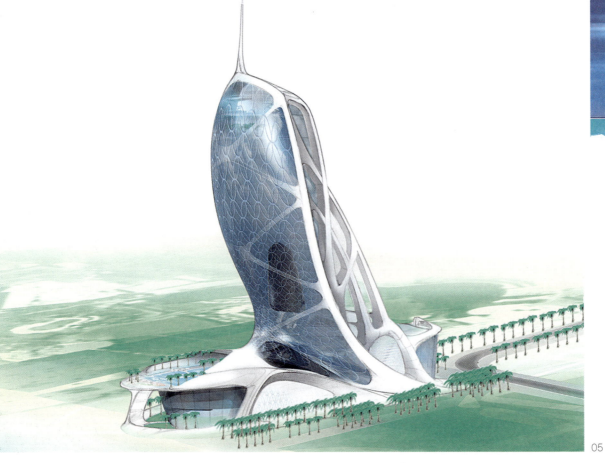

04~
Rendering of the Hydropolis complex for Oman.

05~
A drawing of the Dubai land station shows an elongated structure with a tower that accommodates luxurious apartments.

06~
The plan for Hydropolis Dubai follows the fluid, dynamic forms of its maritime environment.

07~
Cross section showing a semi-natural underwater world with numerous bridges, tunnels and platforms that provide a fascinating view of the surroundings.

06

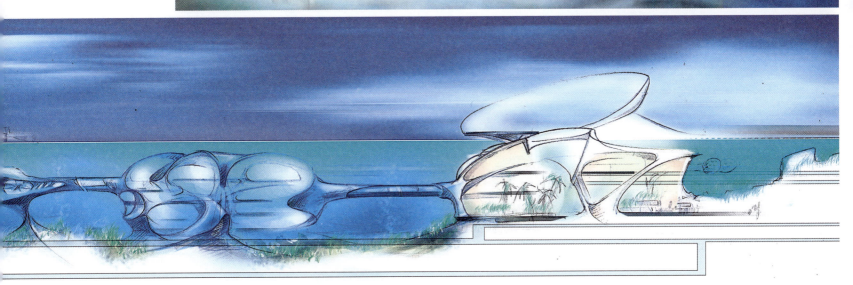

Chalet TOUCH
Porto Sant'Elpidio, Italy

Architect~
Nothing Studio/
Enzo Eusebi

Client~
Gogan

Consultants~
F. Varese, P. DeAngelis,
Y. Consorti

Manufacturer~
Sistema Tetto

Total surface (m²)~
450

Completed~
2005

Website~
www.nothing.it

Photography by
P. Savorelli

Beachlife~
Hospitality

Parked on the beach at Porto Sant'Elpidio in the Italian province of Ascoli Piceno, the rolling form of beach café Chalet TOUCH resembles the caterpillar treads of a giant tank that's halted in mid-crawl. The structure rests on a wooden platform which blends into its side walls, curving up and over the café to become the roof. A bold aesthetic enhances the continuous form of the loop and reflects the café's natural setting, aided by a slatted skin of timber. Open on both sides, Chalet TOUCH features a glass-fronted volume that not only houses both kitchen and café, but also defines the internal parameters of the venue. A rather ghostly interior, which accentuates the airy atmosphere of the café, is furnished with transparent chairs and orderly rows of tables. An olive tree grows behind a transparent screen. The layout changes with the seasons: in summer, the place opens to become an extension of the beach, and in winter, when outdoor pursuits are less attractive, the ambience is cosier and more sophisticated. Intended by the designer to create a link to the sense of the temporary and the transient—a feeling that traditionally characterizes seaside architecture—the building has a cyclic nature that welcomes visitors year round, regardless of the weather.

01~
A glazed façade can be opened to draw the Adriatic breeze into the beachside café.

02~
An olive tree growing inside the café is partitioned off by a transparent screen.

03~
The rolling form of Chalet TOUCH, a design by Italian outfit Nothing Studio, rests on a wooden base.

01

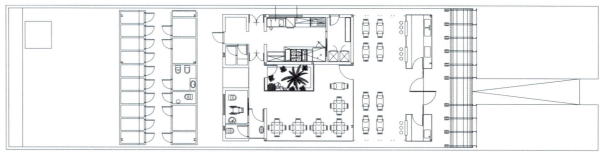
Floor plan

02

03

Architect~
Sebastián Irarrazaval

Contributors~
Ximena García Huidobro
Francisco Ibáñez
Patricio Poblete

Clients~
Olivier Potart
Ana Ibáñez
Hernán Jofré

Structural engineer~
Luis Soler

Graphic design~
C-Proyecta

Total floor area (m²)~
1680

Total cost (US$)~
4 million

Completed~
December 2006

Website~
www.sebastianirarrazaval.com

Photography by
Cristobal Palma

Situated along the maritime passage of Puerto Natales, Sebastián Irarrazaval's Indigo Patagonia Hotel—designed to be explored as a continuous series of steps—offers a Scandinavian-style interior that is as much at one with nature as the nearby Torres del Paine National Park. Guests moving horizontally and vertically through the six-floor hotel follow an architectural choreography that evolves from a gradually ascending ramp on the ground floor to include a system of staircases, corridors and bridges that create fragmented views of public spaces: Irarrazaval refers to the hotel's 'inner void'. An earthy retreat, Indigo Patagonia greets guest with a red-and-black façade of corrugated steel, a material selected to provide continuity between the hotel and buildings throughout the rest of the town.

Inside, however, industrial materials have been exchanged for materials and finishes far closer to nature, such as towering eucalyptus screens in the hotel's communal areas and horizontally installed pine panelling in the bedrooms.
Utilizing every centimetre of available space and taking advantage of scenic vistas in all directions—Balmaceda Glacier and Balmaceda Mount view with the Patagonia Sea—Irarrazaval's boxy building is capped by a rooftop spa. The pine-panelled spa is sliced in two by glazing and includes three outdoor Jacuzzis.
Homage to the town's seafaring vessel Navimag, graphic design for the project was inspired by the iconography of maritime ships and containers.

01~
In the hotel lounge, guests use the internet facilities or sit on comfortable sofas while enjoying a cup of coffee.

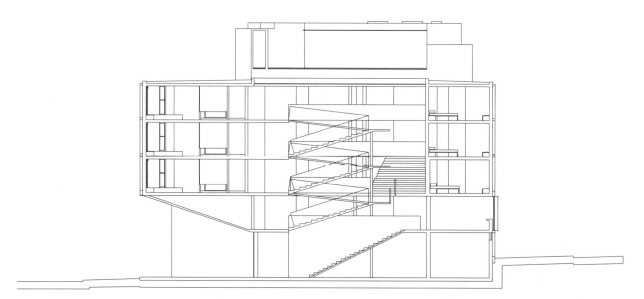
Section

Beachlife~
Hospitality

Indigo Patagonia Hotel
Puerto Natales, Chile

02

Beachlife~
Hospitality

Project~
Indigo Patagonia
Hotel
Puerto Natales, Chile

03

02~
Architect Sebastián Irarrazaval opted for an exterior of timber and corrugated steel, materials that harmonize with those used on other buildings in the vicinity.

03~
A rooftop spa with outdoor Jacuzzi offers a serene view of the Balmaceda Glacier.

04~
An old Patagonian-style house next to the hotel accommodates the Indigo Patagonia Restaurant and Lounge.

05~
Footbridges are one way to access hotel rooms.

Nestlé Bar
Montreaux, Switzerland

Designer~
Fulguro

Client~
Nestlé Suisse

Collaborator~
Swissmate

Manufacturer~
Pasche et Dubath Escaliers

Total floor area (m²)~
256

Completed~
June 2006

Website~
www.fulguro.ch

Photography by
Geoffrey Cottenceau

Beachlife~
Hospitality

Held annually in early June on the shores of Lake Léman, the Montreaux Jazz Festival is Switzerland's best-known music event. For the 40th anniversary of the festival, Nestlé asked multidisciplinary practice Fulguro to design a bar and restaurant to cater for hungry musicians and revellers. The structure was to be built on a dock overlooking the lake. Keeping it simple, Fulguro produced what looks like a large beach hut. When open, the back side of the building rises like the wing of a bird to reveal a kiosk, while also creating a canopy for guests waiting to be served. Facing outwards, a second service counter is positioned on the other side of the bar for patrons seated on the terrace. A deck directly in front of the restaurant, furnished with tables and chairs for dining, extends to form a platform between dock and lake. At the end of the deck, descending towards the water, tiered seating offers undisturbed views of central Europe's second-largest freshwater lake. Easily dismantled, the whole construction was designed to be rebuilt and used at future festivals.

01~
Polycarbonate panelling sporting digitally cut vinyl decals covers the skeleton of the Nestlé Bar, which is made of white-painted pine.

02~
The prefabricated sections of the timber framework were assembled on site. The structure is easy to dismantle and store for further use.

01

03~
One prefab section of the house functions like the lid of a cardboard box; when open, it creates a sheltered area for customers waiting to be served.

04~
Fulguro's Nestlé Bar resembles a beach hut.

05~
Nestlé Bar rests on a platform that extends from the shore of Lake Léman out over the water, ending in steps that provide extra seating and nearly allow visitors to dip their toes in the lake.

06~
Visitors enter the terrace through a fence made from Algues, interlocking plastic modules designed by Ronan & Erwan Bouroullec.

07~
Spotlights mounted on the branches of a tree rising out of the platform illuminate the terrace.

Beachlife~
Hospitality

Project~
Nestlé Bar
Montreaux,
Switzerland

Architect~
Gruentuch Ernst Architects

Client~
Projektgesellschaft Ballastkai

Landscape architect~
Topotek 1

Total surface (m²)~
7264

Designed~
2005

Website~
www.gruentuchernst.de

Renderings by
Gruentuch Ernst Architects

Designed to regenerate an urban area on the eastern shore of Flensburg, Germany, Fördehotel mediates between the past and the future. Gruentuch Ernst Architects' project—which won an architecture competition organized by Projektgesellschaft Ballastkai—resembles an ensemble of harbour warehouses of the type that once typified the country's northern docks. Viewed from the other side of the water, the hotel appears to rise from the depths of the sea, as its powerful vertical lines define the harbourscape. A façade sheathed in a skin of copper—bronze alloy makes the structure looks as though it's been crafted from a bar of gold. Three distinct volumes—each characterized by a pitched roof, footbridges, walkways and decks—extend the external space of the hotel and connect the architecture with the water. Shimmering in the sun and perforated by windows dispersed across its front, sides and sloping roofs, the golden monolith is bathed in translucence. A new landmark, the hotel design exemplifies Flensburg's plans to revitalize this waterside area with high-end offices and residential buildings.

01~
Panoramic view of the Flensburg waterfront from the Baltic Sea.

02~
The architecture of Gruentuch Ernst Architects' Fördehotel was inspired by Germany's traditional waterside warehouses.

03~
Alleys, footbridges, walkways and decks fill the space that separates the three buildings.

04~
Boats can dock right in front of the hotel.

01

Beachlife~
Hospitality

Fördehotel Flensburg, Germany

Doen! Beach Club
Scheveningen, the Netherlands

Designers~
John and Monique de Jong

Client~
Zamen

Total surface (m²)~
960

Completed~
April 2007

Website~
www.zamen.nl

Photography by
Roger Wouters

Restaurant group Zamen, which started with one café and one beach club in 2002, currently runs eight fine establishments all marked by originality, hospitality and quality. Each of the eight has a distinctive identity, however. A beach club called Doen! joined the group in April 2007. Designed by John and Monique de Jong—the couple behind Zamen—the interior is a snow-white space enlivened by the metallic fabrics of cushions scattered across leather sofas. Flower arrangements and an occasional palm tree add a touch of green. An environment in pristine white is perfect for weddings and hen nights, events that regularly take place at Doen! Guests relax on lounge beds, armchairs and banquettes, as well as on chairs outside on the beach; have a drink in the timber-floored beach garden; or enjoy a fireside dinner in the restaurant. Each of these three areas accommodates from 200 to 250 guests. Located in Scheveningen, a popular Dutch resort, the club attracts quite a crowd throughout the summer.

01~
Comfortable armchairs add an aura of exclusivity to lounging on the beach.

02~
Flower arrangements give the interior of Doen! a touch of color.

Beachlife~
Hospitality

03~
Sun worshippers with an aversion to gritty sand can relax in the timbered-floored beach garden.

04~
In the event of bad weather—not uncommon in the Netherlands—a roof can be raised to protect guests sitting in the beach garden.

05~
The restaurant at Doen!—a beach complex designed by John and Monique de Jong—is furnished with luxurious white-leather sofas.

Beachlife~
Hospitality

Project~
Doen! Beach Club
Scheveningen,
the Netherlands

Interior designer~
Absolute Design

Architect~
DPDS

Client~
Fifteen Foundation

Project management~
Noon Projects

Construction~
Midas Construction

Total floor area (m²)~
475

Total cost (£)~
1.1 million

Completed~
May 2006

Website~
www.absolutedesign.co.uk

Photography by
Sam Morgan Moore

Beachlife~
Hospitality

Fifteen Cornwall, UK

Jamie Oliver's Fifteen Foundation has become a global operation, with restaurants in London, Amsterdam, Melbourne and Cornwall. Given the various locations, one might assume that having a seafront dinner at Fifteen surely means eating at the restaurant in Australia. Wrong! Customers in Melbourne settle down for a meal in a cosy basement in the heart of the business district, whereas diners on England's southwest coast enjoy views of a beautiful beach stretching as far as the eye can see. Like the menus of all four restaurants, each unique venue reflects its surroundings. The Cornish branch is no exception. The interior was created by local agency Absolute Design, whose goal was to translate Fifteen's original urban look into an interior relevant to the coastal location, while 'exploiting the contrast between fine dining and a beach hut'. To achieve its objective, Absolute employed a local artist to fuse the urban graffiti aesthetic associated with the original Fifteen in London, with the relaxed Cornish beach culture. Surfers and Olivers beloved Vespa cover kitchen counter and canopy. A banquette running the length of the main dining area overlooks neat arrangements of tables for four, beyond which lie Cornwall's sandy shores. Offset by the bright backdrop, monochromatic furnishings give the restaurant a classic feel, with large globular lights (resembling illuminated buoys) adding a contemporary twist. Diners have unobstructed views of Olivers apprentices hard at work in the open kitchen.

01~
In the summer, the floor-to-ceiling windows are opened to allow a gentle sea breeze.

02~
Tables are fitted with 40-mm thick white Corian tops that represent starched table cloths.

03~
The private dining area is screened off from the rest of the restaurant.

04~
The surrounding walls of the kitchen area are decorated by a local artist.

01

02
03
04

Architect~
xrange

Clients~
The Ambassador Hotel, China Prosperity Development Corp.

Consultant~
Taiwan Construction Research Institute

Total surface (m²)~
25,500

Total cost (US$)~
30 million

Budget per m² (US$)~
1175

Design completed~
2006

Website~
www.xrange.net

Renderings by xrange

Beachlife~
Hospitality

Certain to 'come out on top' with this project, Taipei-based architecture firm xrange has designed a 120-room boutique hotel, complete with international conference facilities, for the peak of the towering mountain range that surrounds Sun Moon Lake. An impressive site that once boasted a residence owned by Chiang Kai-shek, the location commands a vast panorama of the scenery that has made Taiwan's largest lake a popular destination for tourists. Responding to the spectacular views, the designers envisioned a building whose form and situation would offer guests a 360° vista—an experience 'moulded' from the natural boundaries set by slopes too steep for construction and including vast groves of existing trees. Stretched to its maximum, the footprint of the building utilizes the horizontal expanse of the site. The contoured forms of the architecture hover above the treetops, evoking images of geological or meteorological effects akin to swirling clouds or windswept rock striations. Continuously transforming, the geometry of exterior screen walls makes the curvaceous planes of the building appear to revolve. Each floor of the hotel is a prestressed, prefab structural unit. These units are stacked in a seemingly haphazard, organic manner to create generous, sweeping overhangs featuring amenities such as roofed patios, terraces and observation decks.

01~
A foot at one side of the base of the building accommodates an auditorium that opens directly onto decks, offering business people assembled at the hotel for meetings or congresses a momentary escape from lengthy lectures.

02~
Various garden decks are found throughout the hotel. The top 'slab' houses a banquet room, complete with pool and spacious deck.

01

Sun Moon Lake Hotel Nantou County, Taiwan

03~
The simple design of guest-room interiors emphasizes the vast horizontal planes of the lake, visible from the windows. In each room, a sleeping platform extends to become a desk and an eco-friendly fireplace.

04~
View of the reception counter (right) and restaurant (left) of Sun Moon Lake, a Taiwanese boutique hotel designed by xrange.

02

04

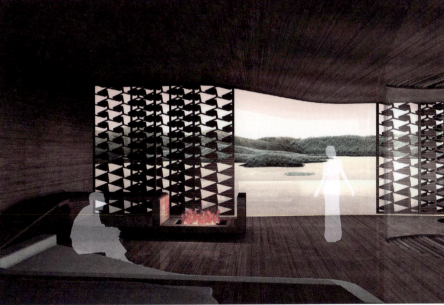
03

Architect~
Concrete Architectural Associates

Client~
IQ Creative

Completed~
July 2006

Website~
www.concreteamsterdam.nl

Photography by
Concrete Architectural Associates

Served with a side order of music, performance and art, the Supperclub on Turkey's east coast is the latest addition to Bert van der Leden's chain of restaurants, famous for providing guests with a unique dining experience. 'Freedom is the keyword at Supperclub,' says entrepreneur van der Leden. 'It's a mix of food, music, performance, art, our staff and... you. An evening at Supperclub has been successful when all five senses have been tickled, so to speak. Supperclub is a free state of sensual experience.'

Asked to create the beachfront sanctum, Concrete, the firm that's collaborated on all projects from the outset—the first Supperclub opened in Amsterdam in 1999—devised a two-part venue, staggered between land and water. Entering through an open-air kitchen located on the upper level, guests are led through olive trees to a platform over the water, which can be used for sunbathing during the day and for dining at night. Turning the idea of a waterbed on its head, Concrete furnished the waterfront space with beds of various dimensions. Circular mattresses, including a golden one reserved for VIPs, fill the gap between the 18-m-long bar and the equally long bed it faces. To maintain the venue's exclusive status and to conceal each night's activities, five vertical projections screens separate the floating deck from neighbouring platforms along the bay. The Turkish Supperclub is shielded from the sun and illuminated at night by screens and pinspots mounted on a white steel construction that covers the upper area and the entrance to the lower tier.

01

02

Beachlife~
Hospitality

Supperclub
Türkbükü, Turkey

01~
One of a chain of similar venues located in spots around the globe, the Supperclub on the Turkish Riviera has a deck that overlooks the Mediterranean Sea.

02~
Resembling giant hats, circular beds arranged beneath straw parasols invite guests to relax in the shade, oblivious to the summer heat.

03~
An accoutrement to alfresco dining is Supperclub's open-air kitchen, which stands amid olive trees and lush greenery.

Architect~
Duangrit Bunnag Architect Ltd.

Client~
Astudo Hotels and Resorts

Completed~
December 2007

Website~
www.designhotels.com/x2resort

Photography by
Oman Mirzaie

A project designed by Duangrit Bunnag to an innovative brief from Astudo Resorts, X2 Kui Buri, an exclusive resort occupying a 3.2-hectare beachfront site on the Gulf of Thailand, consists of 23 units that range from deluxe villas to bungalow apartments. Virtually identical inside, the accommodations derive their auras of individuality from the proximity of each to the bordering terrace, adjacent pool and neighbouring garden areas. Driven by the belief that 'ease, comfort and nature are the only things needed to create a stylish atmosphere that is both visually stunning and incredibly relaxing', Bunnag focused his design on uninterrupted views of the sea, enriched by the interaction between natural light and soft indoor illumination and framed by cleverly applied indigenous materials. Inside and out, spaces flow into one another at X2 Kui Buri; enhancing all these fluid connections are the solid stone walls that determine the hotel's spatial boundaries. Imitating the path of a maze, a wooden boardwalk reveals a different panorama at every turn. An alternative for those who favour a view from the top is a roof terrace that beckons diners in the hotel restaurant to retire 'upstairs' for a nightcap.

01

02

Beachlife~
Hospitality

X2 Kui Buri
Prachuab Khirikhan, Thailand

01~
Each of the 23 units at X2 Kui Buri in Prachaub Khirikhan, Thailand, has a private terrace, and most of these terraces have an ocean view.

02~
Thanks to their pebbled-covered exterior, the villas at X2 Kui Buri merge seamlessly with the solid stone walls on the complex.

03

Beachlife~
Hospitality

Project~
X2 Kui Buri
Prachuab Khirikhan,
Thailand

04

03—04~
The guests have access to private swimming pools.

05~
The 4K restaurant serves fusion cuisine.

06~
X2's late-night bar.

07~
Soft lighting guides guests along pathways throughout the grounds of the X2 Kui Buri resort, which was designed by Duangrit Bunnag Architect Ltd.

Zuri Bar
Knokke, Belgium

Designer~
Gerd Couckhuyt

Lighting design~
Modular Lighting Instruments

Completed~
2007

Websites~
www.interior-gc.be
www.supermodular.com

Photography by
Filip Dujardin

Beachlife~
Hospitality

A word meaning 'white' in Basque and 'attractive' in Swahili, the name of designer Gerd Couckhuyt's new bar precedes itself. Sited in the municipal casino, a familiar landmark in Knokke, a town on the northeast coast of Belgium, Zuri is tipped to become a firm favourite of the country's socialites, who flock to the seaside resort in droves each summer. The venue changes seamlessly from a daytime bar into a nightclub, taking the party indoors, at which point Zuri's white terrace—furnished with Couckhuyt's Moon collection—is sealed off from the interior by curtains. Late callers to the bar enter through a door to the right of the terrace and walk through a darkened tunnel illuminated by fluorescent veins. Guests arriving in the main space, where Couckhuyt's angled ceiling joints create the impression of a cupola, are encapsulated by architecture that 'opens up' after eleven to form one large space, generating a sense of unity between the bar at the front and the club behind it. Two long bars placed back to back reflect the contours of the ceiling. Anchored to these white counters, like ships to a pier, white-polyester stools inspired by female anatomy provide ample bar-side seating. Their curvaceous seats, along with the angular lines of bars and ceiling, are echoed throughout the rest of the interior, including lounge areas and toilets.

Fresh, bright and pure, the white interior at Zuri forms a perfect backdrop for the club's colour-changing lighting system. Developed in collaboration with Modular Lighting Instruments, the manufacturer of Izar, Couckhuyt's purpose-designed puzzle lamp, the lights, like the music, play a decisive role in the carefully orchestrated transition that occurs when the sun goes down.

01~
Because the interior of Zuri is completely white, colour-changing lights are used to create a particular mood—the possibilities are endless.

02~
Rock Mutant features an aluminium frame finished in powder-coated paint. Like all the furnishings at Zuri, this seating element was designed by Gerd Couckhuyt.

01

03~
The Zuri lounger and bar stool, which are part of Gerd Couckhuyt's Moon collection, feature polyester frames and cushions clad in white leather.

04~
Zuri's light jockey uses a VisualDMX light control to generate the desired chromatic atmosphere, adding special effects and dynamics as the evening progresses.

02

03

04

05 06

114 | 115

Beachlife~
Hospitality

Project~
Zuri Bar
Knokke, Belgium

05~
Couckhuyt's lighting designs are manufactured by Modular Lighting Instruments.

06~
Softly rounded polygons are repeated throughout the interior.

07~
Sparking Zuri's nightclub ambience are Couckhuyt's U Shape, Traffic and Bolster luminaires, all by Modular.

Architect~
Waterstudio.NL

Client~
Dutch Docklands

Consultants~
Dutch Docklands,
Royal Haskoning

Engineer~
Royal Haskoning

Total surface (m²)~
22,000

Completed~
Under construction

Website~
www.waterstudio.nl

Renderings by
Waterstudio.NL

Dutch architecture firm Waterstudio.NL has found the perfect solution for those eager to explore their surroundings but reluctant to get their bodies in motion: a tower that rotates one degree each minute and thus 360° in six hours. Commissioned by Dutch Docklands, the floating and rotating structure is scheduled to be erected off the coast of Dubai, although the precise date is a closely guarded secret. The 32-storey, 150-m-high hotel will have 200 bedrooms, six congress rooms and four lifts. Designed in collaboration with the client and with Royal Haskoning, a prominent Dutch maritime-engineering company, the structure—shaped like a dome that tapers to become 'a narrow bullet'—is being touted as an incredibly stable building connected to the shore by means of a floating foundation only 10 m in depth. Constructed from glass and steel, the hotel may be the first to offer rooms with a view that spins—even without the aid of a few drinks at the bar beforehand.

01~
It takes Waterstudio.NL's floating tower—a hotel under construction in Dubai as we go to press—a total of six hours to rotate 360 degrees.

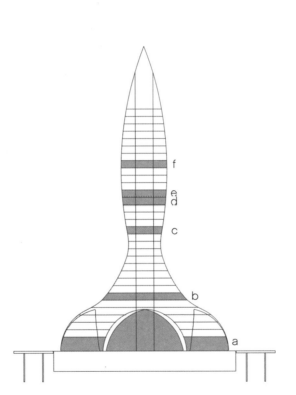

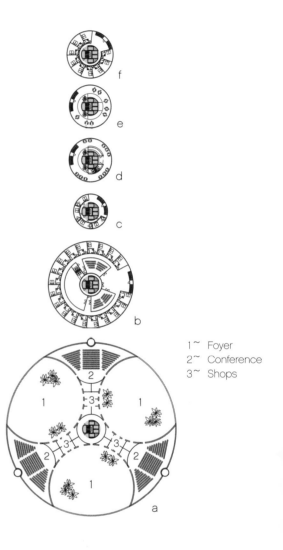

1~ Foyer
2~ Conference
3~ Shops

Beachlife~
Hospitality

Floating and Rotating Tower Dubai United Arab Emirates

Designer~
Heatherwick Studio

Client~
Brownfield catering

Kitchen designer~
Alan Clayton Design

Structural engineer~
Adams Kara Taylor

Steelwork~
Littlehampton Welding

Contractor~
Langridge Developments

Completed~
2007

Website~
www.heatherwick.com

Photography by
Andy Stagg

Beached on the shore at Littlehampton, Heatherwick Studio's sculptural East Beach Café resembles the remains of a gigantic dinosaur, its vertebrae formed by a sequence of thin, steel, vertical slices. Designed to provide the building with both structure and skin, the shell of the eatery carries an air of intrigue, even from behind. Selected for its weathering characteristics, the mild steel used to create this framework is rusting with age, growing in character and allowing the venue to survive all types of weather, fair and foul. The monocoque system that Heatherwick used to construct the East Beach Café—a method in which the skin of a structure supports the load—may seem unconventional, but it's common in the shipbuilding industry and thus suits the location. Dictating the internal space, the undulating exterior penetrates the café, its rippling white walls imitating a fringe of white cliffs. The glass-fronted steel mounds form an architectural cave that protects visitors from the elements, while providing unhampered views over the West Sussex shoreline.

01~
Located on the waterfront, East Beach Café is constantly exposed to saltwater, which increases the oxidation of its shell. Heatherwick deliberately chose steel, realizing that a rusty exterior would add character to the structure.

02~
The shape of the shell is visible in the café's rippling interior wall.

1~ Dining room
2~ Kitchen
3~ Servery
4~ Kiosk
5~ Office
6~ Lobby
7~ Plant
8~ Lavatories
9~ Void

Floor plan

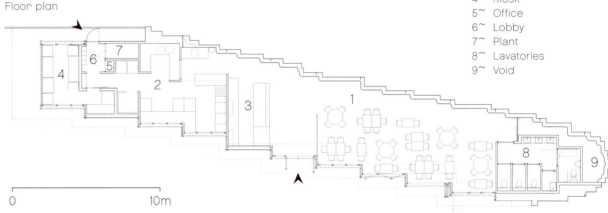

Beachlife~
Hospitality

East Beach Café Littlehampton, UK

03~
The steel shell is not only decorative and protective; it also forms the framework of the building.

04~
Detail of the north elevation.

Sixty Hotel
Riccione, Italy

Architect~
Studio 63 Architecture + Design

Client~
Sixty Group

Manufacturers~
B&B,
Cecchotti,
Danese,
Knoll,
Nord Light,
Tanini

Total floor area (m²)~
1500

Completed~
2006

Website~
www.studio63.it

Photography by
Yael Pincus

Located on the Adriatic coast near Rimini in Riccione—a veritable Mecca for young Italians—Sixty Hotel bears the name of its owner. Redesigned in 2006 by Studio 63, this is the first of four hotels planned by clothing mogul Sixty Group. Housed in new shell, the original 1950s hotel currently sports a white façade pierced by a series of T-bulb-illuminated balconies framed in elegant oval openings. Inside, the organic forms gracing the exterior have been translated into 3D structures, and communal halls boast luminous curved walls that ceaselessly change from one colour and tonality to another. Thirty-nine hotel rooms varying in colour, form and decoration are the work of 30 young artists hand-picked by Studio 63 and Galleria Neon, an exhibition venue in Bologna. Encouraging guests to interact while in the privacy of their own rooms—as well as in the bar, in the restaurant and on the roof terrace—the hotelier has equipped each vivid but minimally furnished room with a webcam: a sassy wink at a generation that's grown up with reality TV and YouTube. The youngsters who gather at Sixty seem anxious to see and be seen—even, or perhaps especially, in the intimate atmosphere of a hotel room.

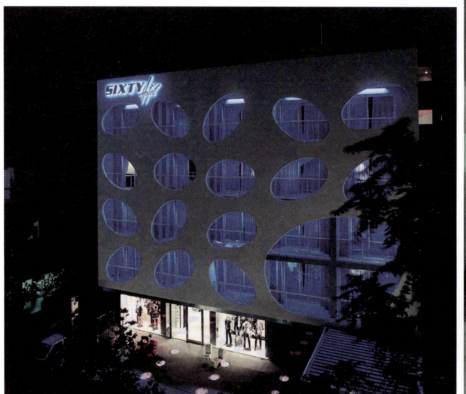

01

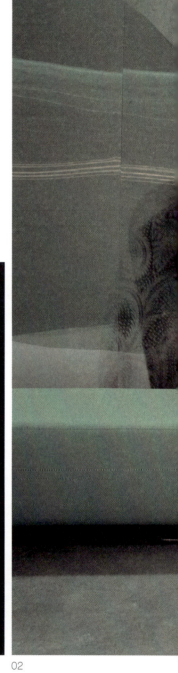

02

Beachlife~
Hospitality

01~
A white skin with oval openings hints at a cartoonish world, while simultaneously giving the building an extreme makeover based on very few alterations.

02~
One of four colours—yellow, green, orange and black—determines the atmosphere of each floor of the hotel.

03~
The Sixty Hotel boasts a stylish reception area.

04~
Thirty young artists contributed to the interior design of the hotel rooms, which greet guests with everything from wall installations and murals to webcams.

05~
The roof terrace overlooks the Adriatic Sea.

03

04

05

Architect~
Concrete Architectural Associates

Scheduled completion~
2009

Website~
www.concreteamsterdam.nl

Photography by
Concrete Architectural Associates

B20 Singapore

Beachlife~
Hospitality

It is not unusual for brainstorming sessions to occur over a few drinks, but for Dutch firm Concrete it was the actual beer and the process of brewing it that inspired the outfit's B20 beer pavilion, located in Singapore. Forming the basis of both the food-and-beverage concept and the architecture, foam—the hallmark of a perfect pint—was reinterpreted and magnified to produce a building that lives and breathes beer at every level. Like the imprints left in a frothy brew after the first sips, openings in the porous membrane that wraps the exterior walls reveal the interior of the building. Inside, suspended from the ceiling of the top floor, Eero Aarnio's transparent Bubble chairs embellish a relaxing lounge area. The architecture of the three-level pavilion, whose top storey is a rotated repetition of the entrance level, creates terraces on the outside of the spherical structure, with spectacular views of the city and surprising glimpses into the pavilion's interior. Concrete's all-embracing concept has turned B20 into a trademark as well as a place for dancing, dining and drinking 24 hours a day.

01~
View of the bar area with Bubble chairs.

02~
View of the restaurant area and terrace of Concrete's B20 beer pavilion in Singapore.

03~
The concept, from beer to building.

04~
View of the building.

05—09~
Models

04

05

06

07

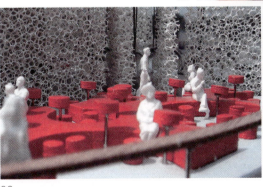
08

09

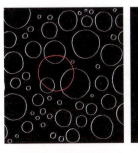

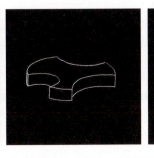
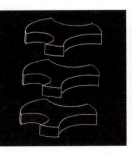

Beachlife~
Art

Art

Ghostnets
Sydney, Australia

Artists~
Virginia Reid,
Jess Poulsen

Client~
Sculpture by the Sea

Materials~
Salvaged fishing nets,
wooden poles

Dimensions~
40 x 40 x 3 m

Completed~
2005

Website~
www.sculpturebythesea.com

Photography by
Clyde Yee

Gone fishing. Caught under giant nets stretched across a patch of Australia's Tamarama Beach, visitors to the 2005 Sculpture by the Sea exhibition were given a preview of what lies beneath the glistening waves visible from shore. A simple construction crafted by Virginia Reid and Jess Poulsen, *Ghostnets* was made from salvaged fishing nets and wooden poles. The artists see their installation—inspired by photos of Southeast Asian fishing nets drying in the sun—as a model of ethical, environmentally responsible creativity. The work addressed environmental concerns and, in particular, those expressed by the WWF Marine Debris Project and its collection of discarded nets, which, left in the sea, kill marine life for years after being abandoned. Aboriginals living in the Northern Territory gathered these nets, which the artists then used to create temporary architectural spaces. Taught by local fishermen to sew the fragments of material together, Reid, Poulsen and a small group of friends sat in sewing circles constructing the *Ghostnets* canopy as if it were an enormous quilt. A makeshift tent hoisted at different heights, on Tamarama Beach the sculpture became a playhouse for adults and children alike.

01

02

01~
Fishermen from Byron Bay, where the artists make their home, taught Virginia Reid and Jess Poulsen how to sew fragments of discarded nets together to make Ghostnets.

02~
The used fishing nets were salvaged in response to the WWF Marine Debris Project.

03~
Visitors to the installation were encouraged to enter the spectral playhouse.

Artist~
Louis de Cordier

Voyage companion~
T.M.C. Volckaert

Exhibition site~
Busan Museum
of Modern Art

Curator~
Manu D. Park

Materials~
EPS foam, fibreglass-
reinforced composite

Completed~
September 2006

Website~
www.louisdecordier.com

Photography by
Louis de Cordier

Artist Louis de Cordier creates modular structures that connect art, architecture and science. His modules provide shelter for the contemporary nomads of our rapidly moving, technology-orientated world. One of his works, entitled Seapod, is an amphibian accommodation for two people. Its two small rooms are accessible through a hatch at the top of the vessel. The module is made from EPS foam sandwiched between layers of a fibreglass-reinforced composite material, a combination that makes it strong and practically unsinkable. On water, Seapod can be steered by standing on it and using one's weight and sense of balance. On land, it can be pulled like a sledge. Starting in the inland waters of South Korea, de Cordier and companion T.M.C. Volckaert sailed the Nam River from Jinju to Busan. At the end of the 220-km voyage, their arrival coincided with the opening day of the Busan Biennale 2006, where Seapod was exhibited.

01~
Sketch of Louis de Cordier's Seapod.

02—03~
Construction of the Seapod.

04~
Day nine on the Nam River: T.M.C. Volckaert and Loui De Cordier on their way to the Busan Biennale.

05~
The Seapod at the Sooyoung Bay yachting centre in Busan, South Korea.

06~
The Seapod arrives in Busan at the end of a ten-day voyage.

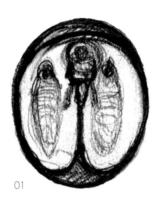
01

02

03

Beachlife~
Art

Seapod, Busan, South Korea

04

Artist~
Florentijn Hofman

In collaboration with~
Jasper van der Made

Client~
International Chamber Music Festival Schiermonnikoog

Dimensions~
8 x 6 x 5 m

Material~
Wood

Completed~
September 2006

Website~
www.florentijnhofman.nl

Photography by
Ilja Sonneveld

Beachlife~
Art

Signpost 5 Schiermonnikoog, the Netherlands

In 2006, three grand pianos appeared to have washed up on the beach of Schiermonnikoog, a Dutch island in the Wadden Sea. The majestic instruments looked as if they had been tossed by the rough waves before landing upside down on the sand, where they waited to be salvaged or to float back to sea on the outgoing tide. The 8x6m piano ensemble, entitled Signpost 5, was the work of Florentijn Hofman, a Dutch artist known for integrating intriguing interactive installations into public space. Hofman had had prefabricated parts transported on a tractor-towed trailer to the beach, where a team of assistants assembled the installation. The timber-clad structures marked the fifth anniversary of Schiermonnikoog's International Chamber Music Festival. During the six days of the festival, the beached pianos were a subject of great interest. Passers-by not only marvelled at their presence but also took advantage of their usefulness. Sitting on the piano legs, visitors to the festival could be spotted peacefully eating sandwiches, snugly sheltered from the wind.

01 & 04~
Hofman's piano seemed to have washed up on the beach with the incoming tide.

02~
The opening ceremony, which introduced Signpost 5 to the Dutch coast.

01

03~
Visitors had mixed feelings about the multifunctional piece, which was art for some and a convenient resting place for others.

05~
View of the three grand pianos lying scattered on the beach.

Ice Fish House
Scheveningen, the Netherlands

Artists~
Satellietgroep, Andries Micke/Mixd Architecture

In collaboration with~
[in] ICE, Blansjaar

Facilitator~
Day of Architecture

Exhibition date~
23 June 2007

Websites~
www.mixd.nl
www.satellietgroep.nl

Photography by
Rop te Riet,
Jacqueline Heerema

In 2007, the theme of the Netherlands' Day of Architecture was Temporary Accommodation. Several artists created works representing two characteristics of the town of Scheveningen, namely subcultures and transience. Members of Satellietgroep and architect Andries Micke built—with the help of several volunteers—a temporary outpost on the beach made from ice and fish. The construction of the Ice Fish House started at one in the morning, and the sculpture slowly melted during the night and the following day when, at four o'clock, nothing was left but a pile of dead fish for the seagulls.

The sculpture was a metaphor for global warming, melting ice caps, changing tides and the subsequent impact on the food chain. It also stood for the possibilities such changes have to offer. Satellietgroep says its installation made 'a statement about the poetry of vulnerability', words that refer not only to the melting sculpture but also to the position of art in and near the sea. The official name of the sculpture was Voorpost Zeedelijk (Zeedelijk Outpost): Zeedelijk is the name of a conceptual 'creative city in or near the sea', where 'art is the first form of life'.

01~
Construction of the Ice Fish House, an installation created by Satellietgroep and architect Andries Micke.

02~
Detail of the sculpture.

01

Beachlife~
Art

Artist~
Barbara Visser

Courtesy~
Annet Gelink Gallery

Dimensions~
120 x 176 cm

Exhibition date~
2002

Website~
www.barbaravisser.net

Photography by
Barbara Visser

Their travel methods are different and their visas nonexistent, but, like tourists, during the summer refugees embark on journeys to the Mediterranean coast. A reference to this duality, Barbara Visser's The world belongs to early risers—a collection of five photographic posters—explores the idea that, despite extensive media coverage of these often fateful voyages, we continue to ignore them. Close-ups of corpses and the injured lying only metres away from unabashed sun worshippers, the images are blatant in their portrayal of human apathy. All that's missing is a speech bubble proclaiming 'Get that body out the way: it's blocking my sun!' A contrast to the scenic postcards usually found along the promenades of coastal resorts, Visser's posters appeared in bus shelters and on billboards around Nice.

01—03~
Five of Barbara Visser's full-colour offset posters have been exhibited in bus shelters and on billboards in Nice, France.

01

02

Beachlife~
Art

The world belongs to early risers, Nice, France

Artist~
The Glue Society

Facilitator~
Sculpture by the Sea Festival

Manufacturer~
Studio Kite

Materials~
Polystyrene, urethane

Dimensions~
150 x 500 x 500 cm

Exhibition dates~
1—18 November 2006

Website~
www.gluesociety.com

Photography by
Jim Parry,
Derek Henderson

Every year in Australia, the Bondi to Tamarama coastal walk serves as a backdrop for the Sculpture by the Sea Festival. In 2006, the tenth anniversary of the event, 108 artists from all over the world showed their work. Free to the public, the festival attracted over 400,000 visitors. One participant was The Glue Society, a creative collective of writers, designers, art directors and film directors that called its melting ice-cream van Hot with the Chance of a Late Storm. The humorous sculpture was the collective's attempt to focus attention on the effects of global warming. The Glue Society's installation received a great deal of attention as well as two prizes: The People's Choice Award and The Kids' Choice Award.

01—02~
The Glue Society designed its melted ice-cream van to demonstrate the effects of global warming.

01

Hot with the Chance of a Late Storm Sydney, Australia

Initiator~
Satellietgroep

Facilitator~
Kunstvlaai

Exhibition date~
6—14 May 2006

Website~
www.satellietgroep.nl

Photography by Satellietgroep

In January 2006 Dutch artists' initiative Satellietgroep established Satellieteiland, an art(ificial) island in the North Sea that serves as a platform for developing a cultural scenario for the future. In May of the same year, artists, students, scientists and day-trippers visiting the coast were invited to participate in a Satellietgroep project called Fles_en_Post (loosely translated: Message in a Bottle). Participants were asked to submit ideas for a cultural service, strategy or product relevant to Satellietgroep's expedition from the mainland to Satellieteiland. The concept was to be placed in a watertight bottle and sent to Kunstvlaai, an alternative art fair that hosted the results of the project. The entries were exhibited at the fair, which was held in May 2006 in and around a converted factory building on the grounds of the Westergasfabriek in Amsterdam. Fles_en_Post is a perfect example of Satellietgroep's attempt to focus attention on the sea as a source of cultural activities involving both artists and the general public.

01~
The poster announcing Fles_en_Post called upon artists, scientists and other interested parties to submit ideas for an expedition from the Dutch mainland to Satellieteiland.

02~
Floris Kruidberg tucked this message into a bottle: 'It would be great if a two-way current existed between the mainland and Satellieteiland; you could float on your back both coming and going.'

01

Beachlife~
Art

Fles_en_Post Amsterdam, the Netherlands

Artist~
Rebecca Horn

Materials~
Steel tower, neon lights, audio equipment

Dimensions~
1060 x 517 x 517 cm

Completed~
1992

Website~
www.rebecca-horn.de

Photography by
Rebecca Horn / VG-Bild Kunst

The Wounded Falling Star, an installation by German artist Rebecca Horn, stands on Barcelona's beach as a monument to restaurants destroyed in the redevelopment of this part of the city prior to the 1992 Olympic Games. A stack of steel cubes rising like a tower of small cafés salvaged from demolition, the structure resembles a multistorey sand castle, its layers precariously balanced one atop the other. Weathered, rusting and elevated on a concrete platform—perfect for sunbathing—the empty volumes, with windows front and back, frame views of the sea beyond. The installation is equipped with neon lights and sound equipment, which make it a visible and audible seaside attraction after dark, when many of the surrounding buildings are rendered invisible by the night sky. Horn's accompanying poem pays homage to the history of her installation:

01~
The stacked steel cubes of Rebecca Horn's art installation mourn the loss of buildings destroyed to make room for the 1992 Olympic Games in Barcelona.

02~
Lights inside Horn's work, The Wounded Falling Star, turn the tower into a beacon after dark.

01

A one way elevator going up,
the seventh room in the
Hotel Peninsular.
No. 414 a place of light and fire.
7 April 1992, Barcelona.
Bursting night upside down.
Flashes of lightning shooting out
of the wounded earth,
penetration of endless rain
neither parachutes nor umbrellas
give protection.
A lighthouse in the night,
its light wanders quietly over
the horizon,
casting our gigantic shadows
over mountain and sea.
Light ejaculated energy,
signs of revolt from the tip of
the steel tower.

Beachlife~
Art

The Wounded Falling Star Barcelona, Spain

Artist~
Florentijn Hofman

Production~
Le Lieu Unique and
the Biennale Estuaire

Dimensions~
20 x 26 x 32m

Materials~
Inflatable, rubber-coated
PVC; pontoon, generator

Completed~
2007

Website~
www.florentijnhofman.nl

Photography courtesy of
Florentijn Hofman

Beachlife~
Art

The fact that Florentijn Hofman is not your average gallery-exhibited artist should be obvious. The world is a huge playground, and he can choose just about any spot in which to display his installations. On this occasion, the Loire River in France was the starting point of a project that ultimately became a gigantic rubber duck. Measuring 26 m in height, it may look like the favourite toy of Sesame Street's Ernie, but it's too big to fit into anyone's bath—and impossible to ignore. From a distance, the creature is little more than a yellow dot on the horizon.

As you get closer, however, it seems to fill the sky. Joining the crowd on the riverbank, you gaze up in astonishment at the immense bird politely nodding its rubber head.

According to the artist, Rubber Duck crosses all boundaries with ease, does not discriminate and is not a political beast. What's more, Hofman's friendly floating fowl has healing properties: it can both define and relieve world tensions. A soft, friendly playmate suitable for all ages.

01~
Gigantic Rubber Duck splashes in the St. Nazaire harbour.

02~
Florentijn Hofman's Rubber Duck in front of a World War II submarine bunker, creating a striking contrast to this solemn reminder of the past.

01

Rubber Duck
Loire River, France

Initiator~
Satellietgroep

Food artists~
René Jansen,
Joost Nieuwenburg

Launch date~
20 July 2007

Websites~
www.satellietgroep.nl,
www.jansen-josten.nl

Photography by
Satellietgroep

Beachlife~
Art

S.MAG is a magazine featuring art by and in the sea. It is published by Dutch artists' initiative Satellietgroep and distributed in the Netherlands in the summer, when coastal activities are in full swing. Various artists, designers, architects and scientists are invited to contribute to each issue, providing they share Satellietgroep's passion for the sea. The magazine covers all sorts of transdisciplinary approaches to the study of the sea and its cultural significance.

On 20 July 2007, the first issue of S.MAG was launched in the canteen of the Scheveningen fish market: an appropriate location for this special event. In keeping with the content of the new publication, food artists René Jansen and Joost Nieuwenburg prepared a seafood-tasting menu for the guests.

01~
Cover of the first issue of S.MAG, a Dutch publication launched on 20 July 2007.

02~
The S.MAG launch was held in the canteen of a Scheveningen fish market in a formerly neglected area of town that is currently undergoing revitalization.

03~
Food artists René Jansen and Joost Nieuwenburg prepared a seafood-tasting installation that featured seaweed as the main ingredient.

04~
Guests at the S.MAG launch were offered four mini courses, all part of a specially prepared seafood menu.

01

S.MAG Launch Scheveningen, the Netherlands

02

03

04

Bondi Beach/21 Beach Cells
Sydney, Australia

Beachlife~
Art

Artist~
Gregor Schneider

Facilitator~
Kaldor Art Projects

Total floor area (m²)~
336 (16 m² per cell)

Exhibition dates~
September—October 2007

Website~
www.gregorschneider.de

Photography by
Gregor Schneider/
VG Bildkunst Bonn

Life's a beach... or is it? Encouraging Australians to consider the openness of their society and the freedoms and liberties they take for granted as citizens of the 'Land Down Under', artist Gregor Schneider created Bondi Beach/21 Beach Cells, an installation aimed at prompting a broader debate on current issues surrounding freedom, immigration, terrorism and asylum. A complex of 21 identical cells, each measuring 4 x 4 m and constructed from standard Australian fencing material, Schneider's structure imprisoned a section of Sydney's Bondi Beach within a uniform grid. A contrast to the relaxed coastal surroundings and normal haphazard arrangement of beach towels and parasols, the installation featured cramped cubicles furnished with matching parasols, airbeds and rubbish bags. Having entered the grey maze, beachgoers found themselves enclosed in spaces that evoked dark associations of detention centres and disharmony. An ironic twist of fate designed to get people to take a walk in the shoes of those less fortunate, the installation—unlike the reality of prison—permitted occupants to enter and exit the confines of their own free will. Erected in September 2007, Bondi Beach/21 Beach Cells sentenced the popular recreational area to a three-week stretch inside Schneider's cells, courtesy of Kaldor Art Projects, the charity that commissioned the work.

01~
The installation consisted of 21 identical cells, each measuring 4 x 4 x 2.5 m.

02~
Each cell was equipped with two doors, but closing certain doors forced those inside to exit the same way they entered, retracing their steps as if caught in a labyrinth.

03~
Each cell was equipped with a parasol, an airbed, and a rubbish bag.

04~
Gregor Schneider wanted his art project to remind Australians of the freedom they enjoy, a privilege unknown to many of the world's less fortunate citizens.

05~
The cells, a grim reference to imprisonment, made a stark contrast to the sunny beach and its ordinarily relaxed atmosphere.

Artist~
Melle Smets

Consultant~
Jeroen Everaerts

Manufacturers~
Kroko Schilte,
Jur van Diggele

Materials~
Wood, canvas

Dimensions~
13 x 10 x 3 m

Exhibition dates~
15—24 June 2007

Website~
www.mellesmets.nl

Photography by
Melle Smets

A petrol station rising from the depths of the sea. Not the view one usually has when sitting quietly on the beach, watching the sun go down. This is clearly the work of an artist with a message. Melle Smets plucked the concept of the petrol station from its ordinary environment and placed it amid the waves to highlight its iconic quality. Smets sees the petrol station as a gateway to a parallel culture created by a worldwide web of motorways and airports and based on similarities in architecture, products and pictorial language across the globe. It's a language well known to 21st-century travellers, who would get nowhere without oil. Adrift against the horizon, the little building and its colourful lighting are symbols of an industrialized society. The occasional speedboat passing by can't fill up at this petrol station, however. In addition to the lighting, the structure is simply a timber frame covered with canvas. The entire construction kit used to build Tentstation measures 13 x 10 x 3 m and is light enough to be easily transported to waterfront sites all over Europe.

01—05~
Tentstation seems to fade into the horizon with the changing of the tide.

01

Beachlife~
Art

Tentstation Wadden Sea, the Netherlands

Artist~
Theo Jansen

Materials~
Plastic tubes

Completed~
Ongoing

Websites~
www.strandbeest.com
www.loekvanderklis.com

Photography by
Loek van der Klis

In 1990, a newspaper column that Theo Jansen wrote for a Dutch newspaper, *de Volkskrant*, led to over a decade and a half of experimentation with mobile creatures made from PVC tubing. Jansen's kinetic sculptures, which can occasionally be seen perambulating the Dutch seafront, are known as *Strandbeesten* or, in English, *Beach Animals*. They were featured in Defining Innovation, a BMW television ad campaign for South Africa, and they received the Jury's Special Prize for Interactive Art at the Arts Electronica Festival 2005. Although *Beach Animals* have no digital or electrical components, their success is due partly to Jansen's scientific background, which included seven years of university-level science studies. Among other things, the artist relies on computer algorithms to establish the best methods for creating the animals' movements. A multiple-limbed Jansen sculpture installed on the beach and powered by the wind resembles a giant skeleton clambering along the shoreline.

01

02

Beach Animals (Strandbeesten)

01~
The founding father of Theo Jansen's Animaris Percipiere family—a group with sensory organs that prevent them from drowning—is Animaris Percipiere Primus, which measures 3 x 10 x 2 m.

02~
Animaris Percipiere has a heavy body that rests on wheels.

03~
Another member of Jansen's Animaris Percipiere family.

Festival of Light
Blackpool, UK

Design concept~
Festival of Light,
part of the Blackpool
illuminations

They Shoot Horses Don't They?
Artist~
Michael Trainor

Lighting programmer~
Greg McLenahan

Completed~
Autumn 2005

Kaleidoscopia
Artist~
Andy McKeown

Manufacturer~
Sanyo

Completed~
August 2007

Website:
www.festivaloflight.co.uk

Photography by
Margaret Clough,
Peter Naylor,
Andy McKeown

Famous for its brightly lit promenade, Blackpool's illuminative history began in 1879, when 100,000 people descended on the English coastal town for the inaugural display of eight electric arc lamps—possibly the world's first electric streetlights—manufactured by Siemens. Keen to revive the town's image as a pioneer of technology and lighting, in 2005 Blackpool Council launched the Festival of Light, a fusion of art and light created to enhance the town's traditional 66 nights of illumination. For the first year of the festival, the team illuminated an existing structure, artist Michael Trainor's They Shoot Horses Don't They?—the world's largest mirror ball, whose name honours Sydney Pollack's film about a Depression-era dance marathon and Blackpool's associations with ballroom dancing. Evoking images of 70s-inspired décors and disco dancing, the revolving orb was lit by six computer-operated moving headlighting units: the control system functioning remotely. The 15-minute light show was repeated throughout the evening, ending at midnight. Two years later, new-media artist and software designer Andy McKeown introduced the beachfront site to Kaleidoscopia, an outdoor installation consisting of a participatory interactive and real-time projected light kaleidoscope. McKeown invited members of the public to download free software which could be used to submit images to be 'kaleidoscoped'. After converting the selected images into large-format displays, he projected them onto a board on Blackpool's North Promenade. Not your average roadside sign, his work illuminated the night with a sequence of dynamic patterns.

01~
Projected image of jelly beans: Kaleidoscopia.

02~
Several projected images, part of Kaleidoscopia.

03—04~
At the Festival of Light in Blackpool, the world's largest mirror ball served as a canvas for a repetitive 15-minute light show.

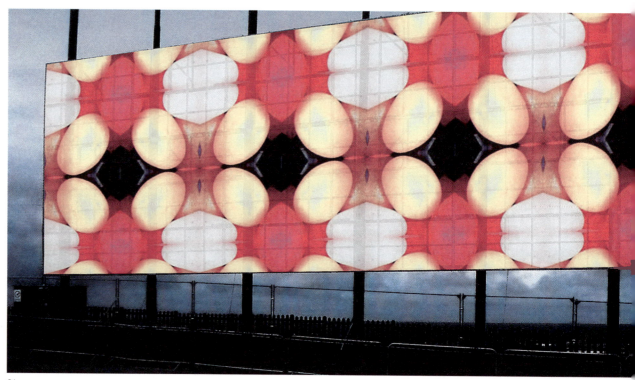

01

Beachlife~
Art

Nomade
Antibes, France

Artist~
Jaume Plensa

Material~
Painted stainless steel

Completed~
June 2007

Website~
www.richardgraygallery.com

Photography courtesy of Richard Gray Gallery

Beachlife~
Art

A contemplative soul sitting on the promenade of Antibes—a busy tourist town in southeast France—Jaume Plensa's Nomade is a sculptural symbol of the unconscious mind. Installed on this patch of the Mediterranean shore in 2007, the 8m high stainless-steel structure—in the form of a seated man—is made from a continuous white mesh of upper-case letters, which represent the artist's exploration of language, spirituality, individual and collective memory. Giving substance to the intangible and ephemeral, Nomade imbues the human condition with physical weight and volume. Viewers who approach the sculpture for a closer look can peer through—or enter—the latticed figure and see fragments of the coastal landscape framed like pieces of a three-dimensional puzzle. As he cradles his legs, the faceless giant's thoughts are left open to interpretation.

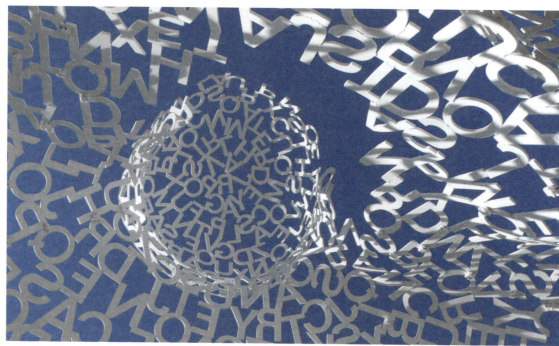
01

02

01~
White stainless-steel letters forming Jaume Plensa's Nomade as seen from inside the sculpture—a latticed figure with an opening that invites visitors to enter and explore the work.

02~
Gazing at the water from the beachside promenade, Nomade sits clasping his knees.

Architect~
Anderson Anderson Architecture

Completed~
2006

Website~
www.andersonanderson.com

Photography by
Anderson Anderson Architects

Oozing from the entrance of After the Flood: Building on Higher Ground—the pavilion that Anderson Anderson erected at the 2006 Venice Biennale—was the architects' green—striped Alluvial Sponge Comb, an installation resembling a mass of enormous elongated watermelons. Bound into sections and punctured by rows of silver eyelets, the spongy structure welcoming visitors to the US pavilion was a sample of the architects' submission to a competition for flood control in New Orleans. An alternative to traditional forms of coastal protection, Anderson Anderson's waterfront proposal accommodates and celebrates the type of extreme weather conditions that have had disastrous effects in both the USA and the city of Venice. Fabricated from layers of waterproof material that vary in rigidity, and designed to be placed in the Mississippi River, the Alluvial Sponge Comb provides flood and erosion control, in part by slowing the flow of water along the riverbank and capturing silt, which aids in the build-up of the shoreline and thus helps sustain life on land and in the water. The creature's giant absorbent tentacles swell as the water level rises and slowly deflate as flooding subsides, releasing vapour back into the environment and reverting to their original shape. On dry land, at the Giardini di Castello, the soft fingers quickly became an outdoor sofa for exhausted visitors to the Biennale.

01~
Visitors to the US Pavilion at the 2006 Venice Architecture Biennale used Anderson Anderson Architecture's green-striped Alluvial Sponge Comb as an outdoor sofa.

02~
Building the installation. Deflated, the Alluvial Sponge Comb is easy to transport.

01

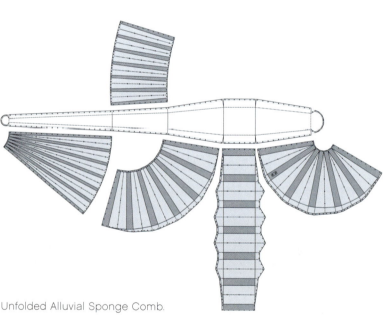

Unfolded Alluvial Sponge Comb.

Beachlife~
Art

Alluvial Sponge Comb Venice, Italy

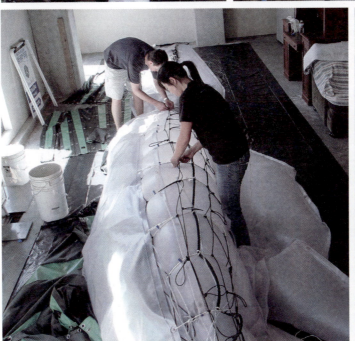
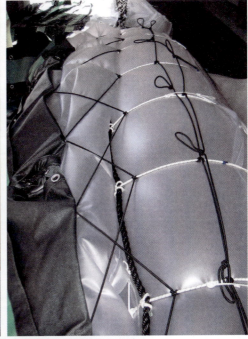
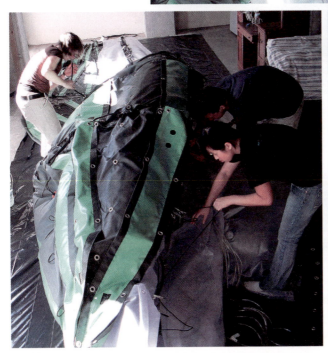
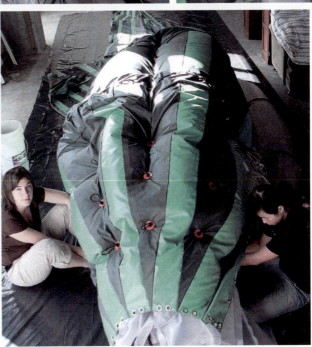

Artist~
Zeger Reyers

Exhibition dates~
1998—ongoing

Photography by
Bram van der Rijden,
Maurits van de Laar

Intrigued by the existence of biotopes and small, fragile, harmonious worlds within a much larger and often hostile environment, artist Zeger Reyers immersed a Parisian terrace chair into the estuary of the Oosterschelde River, famed for its mussel beds. From time to time, he dived to inspect and to photograph the process of development, noting that both mussels and other organisms were attaching themselves to the chair. Two years later, in 2000, Reyers pulled up the first of a series of Mussel Chairs and steamed the entire mussel-encrusted piece in a giant pot designed especially for the occasion. He served the contents to an enthusiastic public. Since then, the artist has held a Mussel Chair performance each year, an event that ends with satisfied diners and absolutely no leftovers. An added bonus is the tax deduction that Reyers can claim on his diving gear, which he uses professionally for 'underwater gardening'.

01~
During the growth process, various organisms attach themselves to the chair.

02—03~
The project is completed when Reyer's Mussel Chair is consumed by diners.

04~
After two years the chair is retrieved from the water.

05~
The fully grown Mussel Chair.

01

02

03

Beachlife~
Art

Mussel Chair Oosterschelde, the Netherlands

04

05

Artists~
Ellie Nuss, James McDermid

Client~
Sculpture by the Sea

Dimensions of each letter~
150 x 150 x 150 cm

Completed~
2006

Photography by
Adrian Lander

Two small words that can determine the nature of an artist's practice, for Ellie Nuss and James McDermid More/Less became the work itself. Selected from the duo's small-scale studies of word pairs—featuring three-dimensional letters adapted to reveal multiple meanings when viewed from different angles—More/Less was enlarged, reinforced to support the weight of several adults and to withstand gale-force winds, and presented at Sydney's 2006 Sculpture by the Sea exhibition. Each letter was crafted from a 1.5 m² cube.

The sculpture analysed alternative ways of seeing and thinking as one navigates the environment, thus stimulating both the experience and the process of creative thinking. As well as its original intent—as a contribution to an Australian art exhibition—the structure raised some interesting questions about the contrast between this stretch of natural coastline and the encroaching urban sprawl. The work, which emerged from a labour—intensive process that took six months, was awarded the Damon Courtenay Memorial Young Sculptor Prize.

01~
Each 1-m letter is made from a pine frame finished in plywood

02—05~
When viewed from different angles, the three-dimensional letters reveal different words. The artists wanted to stimulate creative thinking by forcing observers to look at their surroundings in new ways.

01

02

More/Less
Sydney, Australia

Beachlife~
Art

03

04

05

Designers~
FriendsWithYou, David Choe, Ara Peterson, Misaki Kawai, Paperrad, Devil Robots, Mumble Boy

Client~
Scion

Manufacturer~
FriendsWithYou

Completed~
2006

Website~
www.friendswithyou.com

Photography by Abraham Kalili

A bobbing line of bold blimps followed a police car along Miami Beach. Part of Art Basel 2006, Skywalkers was not an ordinary police-protected demonstration, however. Designed for the Scion INSTALLATION3 Art Show—a revolutionary scheme promoting independent artistic expression across the USA—the balloons were made by FriendsWithYou, a multidisciplinary studio with headquarters in Miami and New York City. Among the vibrant characters on parade was a flying whale, a toothy dog and a giant striped 'worm'. High as kites and held down by an army of volunteers, the animated figures dipped and swooped along the seafront like fantasy sea creatures drunk on helium. The work of FriendsWithYou, David Choe, Ara Peterson, Misaki Kawai, PaperRad, Devil Robots and Mumble Boy, the blimps bulged against the blue sky, spreading a rainbow of colour.

01~
Eighteen helium-filled balloons bobbed along the beach, guided by 150 volunteers. The giant blimp parade marched to music that FriendsWithYou composed especially for the occasion.

02~
Smiling Malfis, designed by FriendsWithYou.

01

Beachlife~
Art

Skywalkers
Miami, FL, USA

03~
Ara Peterson gave birth to the huge Wrapped Phantasm.

04~
Alien from the Planet Fluffy is the work of Devil Robots, a Japanese outfit.

05~
Fuji-san is Misaki Kawaii's tribute to Mount Fuji.

06~
Neddrix Dogstrum is the brainchild of PaperRad.

07~
David Choe calls this whale of a whale Munko.

08—09~
Another balloon by FriendsWithYou is Grubaba the 'spectrum worm'.

03

04

Beachlife~
Art

Project~
Skywalkers,
Miami, FL, USA

05

Beachlife~
Residential

Residential

Villa Soravia
Millstatt, Austria

Architect~
Coop Himmelb(l)au

Client~
Erwin Soravia

Planning office~
Dolenz

Structural engineers~
B+G Ingenieure,
Bollinger and Grohmann,
Gerolf Urban

Mechanical engineers~
IC-Consult, Wurzer

Total floor area (m²)~
500

Completed~
August 2005

Website~
www.coop-himmelblau.at

Photography by
Gerald Zugmann

Beachlife~
Residential

Villa Soravia, a private holiday residence, lies on the shore of Lake Millstatt, a body of water at the southernmost tip of Millstatt, a health resort in Carinthia, Austria. Adhering to regulations that require a new building to respect the contours of the previous structure and the angle of its roof, the architects at Coop Himmelb(l)au approached the villa as a renovation project. The result, a striking white ensemble, is defined by the original gable roof, an oblique tower, a generously defined exterior and an inimitable spatial structure. Standing on a platform of reinforced concrete, the upper area of the former house has been separated from semi-public spaces at ground level, where floor-to-ceiling glazing on the side facing the street introduces passers-by to the section of Villa Soravia that functions as an exhibition space for local artists. The same degree of transparency is repeated on the residential side of the building, which also features a glass façade. Extending from the living room and forging a connection between the interior and outdoor spaces, a terrace heads towards the lake. From the terrace, a concrete stairway leads to a boxy wooden pavilion perched at the end of an elevated walkway over the water. A concrete path linked to the walkway directs guests to a living room, gallery and television room. Set atop the gallery as an extension of the private accommodation is a tilted tower, which houses the master bedroom, toilets and a generous terrace with views of the lake. Adding a touch of colour to the white structure, a sky-blue stair ascends to a playroom and bedrooms in the children's loft.

01

02

01~
Sicilian olive trees adorn both the interior and exterior of Villa Soravia, enhancing the Mediterranean atmosphere.

02~
The living area is furnished with a table and chairs designed by Coop Himmelb(l)au. Curtains custom designed by Peter Kogler refer to the rippling surface of the lake.

03

Beachlife~
Residential

Project~
Villa Soravia
Millstatt,
Austria

03~
The wine rack at the back of the wine-cellar lounge can ascend through the ceiling to appear in the living room.

04~
Sky-blue stairs lead to the children's loft.

05~
Long curtains can be drawn to separate the bathroom on the upper level from the main bedroom.

Floating House
Chatou, France

Designers~
Ronan & Erwan Bouroullec

Collaborating architects~
Jean-Marie Finot, Denis Daversin

Client~
CNEAI

Dimensions~
23 x 5 m

Total surface (m²)~
110

Completed~
2006

Website~
www.bouroullec.com

Renderings by Paul Tahon, Ronan & Erwan Bouroullec

Beachlife~
Residential

Moored to the L'île des Impressionnistes (Impressionists' Island) at Chatou, Floating House is part of an artist-in-residence project initiated and supported by CNEAI, a French contemporary art centre. Those who spend time in the buoyant studio are invitees and guests of CNEAI. A collaborative project by the Bouroullec brothers and architects Jean-Marie Finot and Denis Daversin, the 23-x-5-m vessel responds with both practicality and panache to the client's brief for a contemporary houseboat-cum-studio to be realized on a modest budget. Provided with only a modest budget, the designers created a sleek houseboat whose aluminium shell—snugly tucked inside lattice-work designed to support a screen of living plants, which will fuse the barge with its verdant surroundings—bobs gently on the waters of the Seine. At night, reflections from the many lights on shore strike the water and bounce back to illuminate the Ipé walls of the interior, one side of which features fenestration that draws an abundance of natural light, a boon to artists, into the rooms during the day. Those inside the barge have splendid views of the serene landscape which inspired Renoir to paint Déjeuner des Canotiers (Luncheon of the Boating Party) in 1881. Being a part of this fanciful atmosphere—an environment so conducive to contemplation and creativity—is sure to bring out the most in any artist-in-residence.

01~
Red-cedar latticework encourages climbing plants to cover the outside of the boat, integrating the vessel into its surroundings and shielding occupants from prying eyes.

02~
Furnishings on the 23-m² deck include chairs by the Bouroullec brothers—Striped (Magis) and Slow (Vitra)—and their Metal Side Table (Vitra).

03~
The floating house by night.

04~
A centrally positioned white wall separates the sleeping area and kitchen from the living area.

01

03

02

04

Architect~
Michael Maltzan Architecture

Total floor area (m²)~
2000

Total cost (US$)~
6.5 million

To be completed~
2011

Website~
www.mmaltzan.com

Drawing and renderings by Michael Maltzan Architecture

Michael Maltzan's Beach House features two volumes: a single bar and, piercing the bar, a tapered form that expands towards the ocean. As one passes through the threshold and into the bar, the building performs like an instrument, maximizing a framed view of the western horizon. The form of the volume extends the visual restrictions of the house to embrace the ocean. This calibrated infiltration is also expressed in the sectional overlap of public beach and private realm, in which sand slips like a carpet beneath the floating mass of the house. The relationship of house to site is substantial yet precise: two dissimilar forms generate an area of circulation shared by building and beach. A slender stairway descends from the built form to the beach floor, while a heavier mass rises from the sand to support the main volume of the house. Orientated towards the distant view, the angular form of the dwelling simultaneously defines twin courtyards, which flank the interior. The resulting morphology creates a consensual relationship between residence and beach and between public and private space, a hybrid manifest in terms of both perceived experience and physical form.

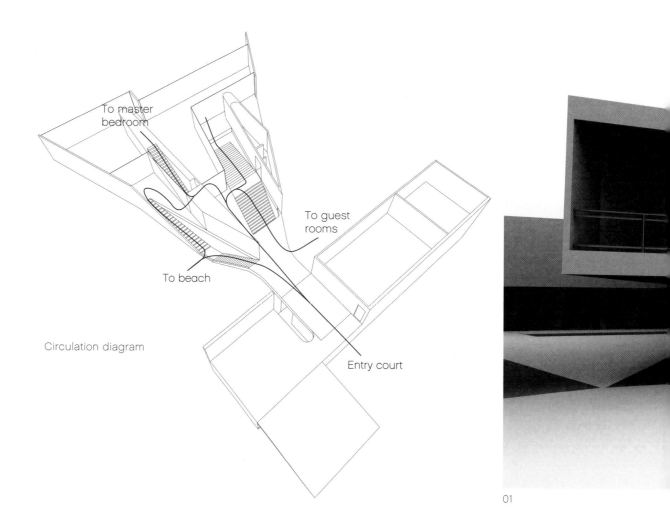

Circulation diagram

01

Beachlife~
Residential

Beach House
Malibu, CA, USA

01~
South elevation, facing the ocean.

02~
Context model.

03~
Southeast elevation.

04~
East façade and courtyard.

05~
Northeast aerial.

02

03

04

05

Architect~
Pezo von Ellrichshausen Architects

Client~
Casapoli cultural centre

Engineer~
Cecilia Poblete

Total surface (m²)~
180

Completed~
2005

Website~
www.pezo.cl

Photography by
Cristobal Palma

Marooned on the side of a cliff overlooking the Pacific, Poli House occupies a rural setting on Chile's Coliumo Peninsula, an area sparsely populated by farmers, fishermen and summer tourists. Functioning as holiday house and cultural centre, the building required an interior that could meet the needs of an informal public space, as well as those of a private dwelling: a layout both monumental and domestic, where aspects associated with either sphere would not negatively affect the other. Consequently, Pezo von Ellrichshausen Architects left the rooms nameless and functionless: empty spaces with varying degrees of connection uniting them. Service functions are organized within an over-dimensioned perimeter inside a thick wall that acts as a buffer. The hollow wall accommodates kitchen, vertical circulation areas, bathrooms, closets and a series of interior balconies. Whenever necessary—to create a large area for cultural events, for example—all furniture and domestic objects can be stored inside the perimeter. The angular structure, built from hand-finished concrete and frames of untreated timber, radiates the warmth of the surrounding landscape.

01~
Poli House is an angular building that serves as both a cultural centre and a summer residence.

02~
A 1-m-thick hollow wall accommodates stairs, circulation areas and living space. It can also be used as a place to store furniture when the building is used as a venue for exhibitions or other events.

01

Beachlife~
Residential

Poli House
Coliumo, Chile

03~
Rooftop terrace.

04~
Poli House has a rough outer surface that blends into the surrounding landscape.

05~
Untreated timber appears throughout the building: in frames, interior surfaces and sliding panels that function as both doors and shutters.

03

178 | 179

Beachlife~
Residential

Project~
Poli House
Coliumo, Chile

04

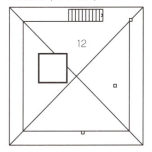

Terrace (NPT+7.65)

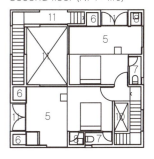

Second floor (NPT+4.10)

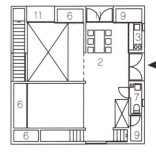

First floor (NPT+1.50)

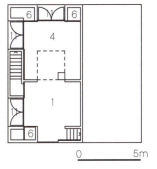

Ground floor (NPT+0.00)

0   5m

N

1~ Living room
2~ Dining room
3~ Kitchen
4~ Studio
5~ Bedroom
6~ Closet
7~ Bathroom
8~ Sink
9~ Storage
10~ Void
11~ Balcony
12~ Terrace

Architect~
Cheng+Snyder

Construction~
W. Eben Greenleaf Jr. Carpenters

Structural engineer~
Structural Integrity Consulting Engineers

Total floor area (m²)~
17

Total cost (US$)~
20,000

Completed~
July 2007

Website~
www.chengsnyder.com

Photography by
Cheng+Snyder

Not your average garden shed, Cheng+Snyder's Writer's Block I is a multifunctional one-room building that combines a writer's studio and boathouse. Referring to the age-old predicament of form versus function, the architects describe the project as a question of 'how much function can be packed into a minimal structure'. They say it's more than simply a matter of utility, pointing out the challenge that goes with 'ecological and political implications in an era of diminishing natural resources'. The result of their deliberations is a structure that is playful, aesthetic and, above all, practical. Located at the mouth of the Sheepscott River in Westport, Maine, the 57 m² block has a deceptive appearance. Although it looks like a monolithic wooden volume at first glance, the building divulges its true identity on closer inspection, when hidden doors open to reveal an entrance, windows and an unexpected space for storing a canoe. Utilizing every centimetre of space, the dwelling features structural studs that double as bookshelves and storage niches, and the surface of the boat compartment can be used as desk or bed. Borrowed from the traditional 'saltwater barn', windows and awnings light the modest interior and maximise views of the river.

01~
Writer's Block I, closed.

02~
Writer's Block I, open. When open, the otherwise hidden doors reveal an entrance, windows and storage areas, while also providing additional views.

03~
Surfaces in the interior can be used for working or sleeping.

01

02

Beachlife~
Residential

Writer's Block I Westport Island, ME, USA

04~
Inside the building, a sliding panel lends access to the boat-storage compartment.

05~
Writer's Block I contains a hidden space for storing a canoe.

06~
Those inside have a 270° view of the water.

The Distributed House
Harbour Island, Bahamas

Architect~
Office for Metropolitan Architecture

Associate architects~
Bruce LaFleur & Associates

Client~
Jane Wenner

Structural engineers~
ABT Arnhem, Rob Nisse

Landscape master planning~
Inside-Outside

Service engineer~
Arup

Website~
www.oma.nl

Photography by
OMA

Beachlife~
Residential

On an exquisite site on Harbour Island in the Bahamas—an area of low dunes, hills, valleys and a partially accessible jungle—OMA's architects have distributed the separate volumes of a residence in such a way that each captures a particular feature of the landscape. Dominating the centre like a mini acropolis is the dining room, a square space with four counterweighted walls that open with ease to transform the volume into a covered area for outdoor dining. The master bedroom perches on the dunes like a Temple of Venus, while the guesthouse faces the sea and an Atelier van Lieshout (AVL) container assembly accommodates the children's room. The pool functions as a connecting unit, and servants' quarters discreetly guard the entrance. The various 'pavilions' are linked by a series of pathways that ensure a golf buggy-friendly route from one part of the house to another on an island that prohibits the use of cars. The Distributed House has direct access not only to the island's pink shores but also to the thick jungle that takes the place of a more ordinary back garden.

01~
The guesthouse, ensconced in a verdant setting, is located near the beach, which is directly accessible via a stairway.

02~
A centrally positioned dining room forms the hub of the design.

01

03 & 05
The children's room is in a container assembly designed by Atelier van Lieshout (AVL).

04~
A view of the site and the various volumes of the Distributed House, which are connected by pathways that cut through the surrounding greenery.

03

184 | 185

Beachlife~
Residential

Project~
The Distributed House
Harbour Island,
Bahamas

04

Architects~
Carlos Ferrater,
Carlos Escura

Client~
Jose Manuel Ferrater

Technical architect~
Benjamin Caballer

Manufacturer~
Construcciones PJ 98

Total surface (m²)~
120

Total cost (€)~
320,000

Duration of construction~
1 year

Completed~
2006

Website~
www.ferrater.com

Photography by
Alejo Bagué

Beachlife~
Residential

For architects Carlos Ferrater and Carlos Escura, Casa de Alcanar represents a visualization of research they have undertaken over recent years: the study of conceptual abstraction in relation to landscape and of the social organization of a dwelling that functions as a system of autonomous elements existing side by side. Laid out as separate bodies, the volumes of this house function independently. Positioned together, however, they form a traditional dwelling. The structure on the eastern side of the building site—intended for use as living room, dining room, larder and kitchen—contains features designed specifically for the current owners, including a mezzanine level with special lighting designed for the display of a collection of primitive art. Opposite this building, another white volume—intended as a cosy retreat—accommodates bedroom, closet space, bathroom, small study and library. Steps on the outside of a third volume, located on the south side of the site, lead to a mirador on the roof, beneath which are another bedroom and bathroom, as well as a studio, all concealed by a latticework façade. Visible through regimented lines of palm trees in the garden, the sea glistens in the Spanish sun, beckoning those inside to enjoy the coolness of its waters.

01~
The site occupied by Casa de Alcanar accommodates three volumes that function as a traditional dwelling,

02~
Ferrater installed a 'library' on the upper part of the bedroom walls.

01

Casa de Alcanar Tarragona, Spain

03~
Helicopter view of the beach-front site.

04—05~
The area between the three structures.

06~
As seen through the window, the garden looks as pristine and orderly as a painting on the wall.

Beachlife~
Residential

Project~
Casa de Alcanar
Tarragona, Spain

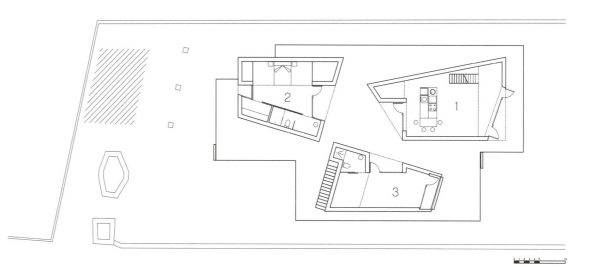

1~ Living room
2~ Bedroom
3~ Guest room

Architect~
Front Architects

Total area (m²)~
Usable: 14.34
Storage: 14.34

Website~
www.frontarchitects.pl

Renderings by
Front Architects

Beachlife~
Residential

Single Hauz Concept

Inspired by single friends, billboards and the living habits of prehistoric man, Front Architects designed Single Hauz, a dwelling that takes compact living to new heights. Recognizing that everyone needs to be alone from time to time, and playing on the seemingly inherent human desire to look down at the world from above, Front Architects put their brainchild on a pedestal. Positioned atop a pole, the 1.8-x-6-m house, which has the potential to occupy any number of locations—from forests and lakes to dense urban jungles—contains living room, kitchenette and bathroom. It holds connotations of childhood tree houses and primitive shelters in the thick canopy of the rainforest. Seen by the designers as an architectural tree trunk, the structural leg accommodates wiring and plumbing for mechanical systems and water supply. Occupants access the house by climbing an exterior staircase, complete with landing, that zigzags in front of the cylindrical support. They can enjoy their trip to the top safe in the knowledge that they are in full view of those below.

01~
The Single Hauz can be placed in any type of environment.

02~
Residents have to climb the zigzag stairs in order to reach their home.

Floor plan

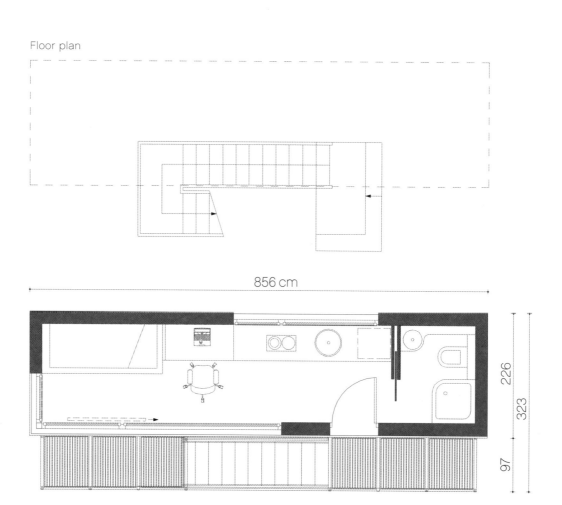

Private Residence
Positano, Italy

Architect~
Lazzarini Pickering Architetti

Service consultant~
Antonino di Maio

Site coordinator~
Michele Cinque

Consultants~
Andrea Biondi,
Isabelle Berney,
Michael Clarke,
Sara Nussberger,
Giuseppe Postet,
Michael Stahlmann

Manufacturers~
Baldieri, B&B Italia,
Boffi, Edra, Flos,
IDCO, Knoll, Lelievre,
Manuel Canovas, Makro,
Rubinetterie Ritmonio,
Villeroy & Boch

Total surface (m²)~
350

Completed~
2004

Website~
www.lazzarinipickering.com

Photography by
Matteo Piazza

Beachlife~
Residential

A private residence in the ancient seaside town of Positano, on the Amalfi Coast, this building designed by Lazzarini Pickering Architetti combines venerable materials and contemporary structures. Interconnecting the dwelling's three floors are four large steel-framed volumes covered in 18th- and 19th-century Vietri tiles. A ceramic ribbon descends 6m from the living-room ceiling, stretches across the floor and juts out over steps to become a table hovering in midair. Hitting the wall, the ribbon reverses direction, creating a canopy gleaming with a series of lamps. A seating area upstairs, nicknamed the 'flying sofa' and clad with Vietri tiles on its underside, cantilevers 2m into the portico area to form an ideal observation post. A wide staircase scattered with cushions and designed to be used as casual seating leads off the living area. Framed by an angular passage in much the same way as the dining room, these stairs lend access to the first floor, where the master bedroom boasts the king of the castle: a large tiled platform supporting both bed and spacious bath. Positioned just off the kitchen downstairs, an alternative to a private indoor bath is a small swimming pool that overlooks the sea.

01~
Hovering 6m above the dining area is a sitting room clad in centuries-old Vietri tiles, a material repeated throughout the residence.

02~
The main living room is visible though 5-m-high, 18th-century arches. Interior walls are decorated with a collection of late 19th-century suzanis (embroidered wall hangings) from Uzbekistan.

01

03~
Soft mattresses on the tiled patio next to the pool.

04~
A small swimming pool with a grand view.

Beachlife~
Residential

Project~
Private Residence
Positano, Italy

05~
A ribbon of ceramic tile descends from the ceiling of the main living room to form a dining table before continuing upwards to hold Baldieri can lights.

06~
A B&B Italia bed, covered with a Manuel Canovas spread, rests on a Vietri-tiled platform that continues to form the bathroom floor.

07~
Cushions and bolsters in the second living room are covered in Lelievre fabric, custom designed by Idco.

Architect~
Rojkind Arquitectos

Client~
Mace International

Consultant~
Office for Urbanism

Structural and bioclimatic engineer~
Arup Agu

Industrial designer~
Esrawe Diseño

Urban research~
MXDF, Ambiente Arquitectos

Submission date~
2007

Renderings by Rojkind Arquitectos

Beachlife~
Residential

Iconic symbols mark Michel Rojkind's competition entry for a marina in Ajman Free Zone, UAE. Resembling a pair of architectural dentures, two white-surfaced towers rising from the paved site in his renderings are what Rojkind calls 'gateway buildings that will be recognized from a distance'—skyscrapers designed to attract the attention of visitors and residents alike. The high jagged volumes pinpoint the spot at which water meets land. Defining and enhancing the experience of users are the low-rise sections of Rojkind's master plan, which are fully integrated with public space and with the urban design of the site. It's here that one can enjoy the marina on a more intimate scale. Pedestrian walkways along the waterfront, as well as those linking the project to commercial facilities, keep sightlines open to provide interesting views while allowing easy access to the various sections of the complex.

Rojkind Arquitectos has also included a necklace of buildings—the Crescent—which is based on the notion that although each volume functions independently, together they form a functional and aesthetic entity. The designers have given each of these structures a unique architectural expression, while making sure that the Crescent remains a unified, recognizable urban structure. All activities in the Crescent relate to the 'platform' of the development, a base whose articulation features an inner courtyard and an external presence to the waterfront. Possessing a level of autonomy granted by its distinctive architecture, the Crescent stands alone and yet is fully interwoven into the urban design.

01~
Windows in the high-rise building are tilted at a 45° angle to emphasize the view of the marina.

02~
Low-rise buildings characterize the Crescent, a feature of the complex containing shops, apartments and parking areas.

03~
The façade of the main building was designed in accordance with an analysis of sunlight at this location, a study carried out to make sure that residents would have sufficient shade.

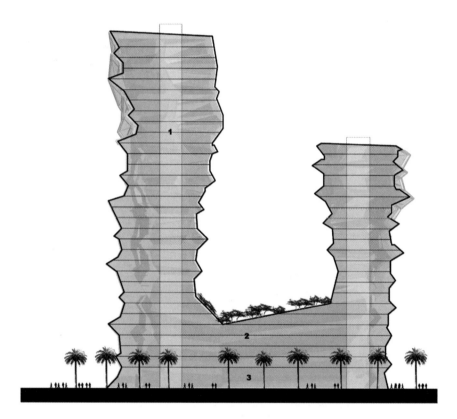

1~ Apartments
2~ Parking
3~ Leisure space

Marina Ajman Free Zone, United Arab Emirates

Architect~
MOS

Client~
Doug and Becca Worple

Engineer~
Bowick Blackwell

Manufacturers~
Kropf Industrial,
Rich Penfold

Total floor area (m²)~
670

Completed~
August 2007

Website~
www.mos-office.net

Photography by
Florian Holzherr

Michael Meredith's Floating House, located on Canada's Lake Huron, is designed to fluctuate with the tide. Drastically changing from month to month and year to year, the dwelling adapts to the ongoing dynamics of Huron's water levels, as it floats atop a structure of steel pontoons. Owing to the logistical problems of working on water, compounded by the remote location of the project, MOS Architects joined forces with Kropf Industrial (specialists in the design and manufacture of floating structures for the aquaculture industries) to develop a prefabricated structure. Steel platforms with integrated pontoons were the first to be built and towed to shore, while the construction crew, taking advantage of Canada's bitter winter, erected the house on the frozen lake. As construction went on, the quintessential houseboat travelled an approximate total of 80 km on the lake before being towed to the site and anchored.

A gangway connected to the rocky shore ushers visitors from land to the structure's upper level. An alternative entrance, which leads to the lower level, is formed by a series of wooden decks positioned over the water. The familiar form of the house—a rectangular box capped by a gable roof—encloses both the interior living space and sections of the exterior. An open platform and large windows at either end of the house provide unobstructed views of the lake and coast. On the sides, replacing windows and giving the residents more privacy, certain slats of the wood-panelled façade have been positioned farther apart to allow light to enter the interior and to let those inside steal glimpses of their idyllic surroundings.

01~
Special features of Michael Meredith's design are an eye-catching, wood-panelled exterior and a gangway that extends from the upper level of the house to a grassy bank at the edge of Lake Huron.

02~
Linked to the shore, several wooden decks poised above the rocky terrain lend access to the house.

01

Beachlife~
Residential

Floating House Lake Huron, Canada

03~
In the living room, four windows frame views of Lake Huron that can be compared to a quartet of scenic photographs.

04~
An open, ground-floor veranda forges a connection between interior and exterior living spaces.

1~ Dock
2~ Bridge
3~ Living area
4~ Kitchen
5~ Office
6~ Bedroom
7~ Bathroom
8~ Sauna
9~ Washroom
10~ Pantry
11~ Storage

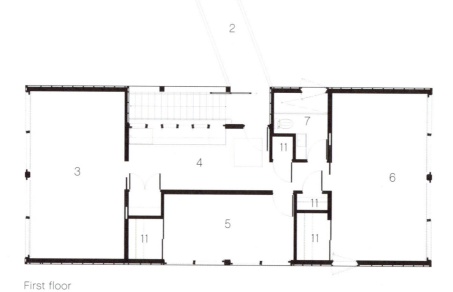

First floor

200 | 201

Beachlife~
Residential

Project~
Floating House
Lake Huron, Canada

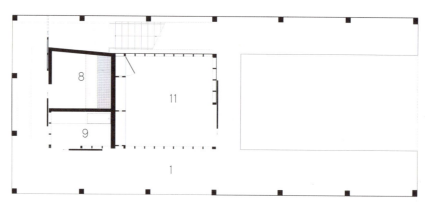

Ground floor

Architect~
Philippe Stuebi
Architekten with
Eberhard Troeger

Landscape architect~
Kuhn Truninger
Landschaftsarchitekten

Completed~
2007

Website~
www.philippestuebi.ch

Photography by
Dominique Marc Wehrli

Facing Mount Pilatus, the giant portholes dotting the façade of this residence in Switzerland—a project by Philippe Stuebi Architekten that took two years to complete—allow occupants to view the imposing landscape through a screen of two-dimensional bubbles. For those outside the house, the apertures frame views of the dual-levelled orangery, living room, guest room and staircase.

On this site of many contrasts, as the bold, concrete-edged fenestration of the main exterior wall turns the corner to meet the building's roughly rendered sides, lush greenery gives ways to majestic views of another Swiss peak, Mount Rigi. Whiteness and transparency continue to predominate inside, where the staircase is guarded by a clear barrier and the living quarters are a model of alabaster. Extending from the rear of the house, half sheltered by the basement and half exposed to the elements, a 25-m-long pool defines the terrace area. A stone's throw away from the lake, a boathouse and concrete jetty provide residents with ample access to the natural waters of Lake Lucerne, as well as with a place to store aquatic equipment.

01~
Model of a residence whose realization took the team at Philippe Stuebi Architekten two years to complete.

02~
A terrazzo floor surrounding the pool continues past the jetted concrete boathouse, which opens into Lake Lucerne.

03~
A stairway lends access to the house, which includes a dual-levelled orangery, living quarters in alabaster, office lounge and a lovely guest room.

02

01

Beachlife~
Residential

O House
Lake Lucerne,
Switzerland

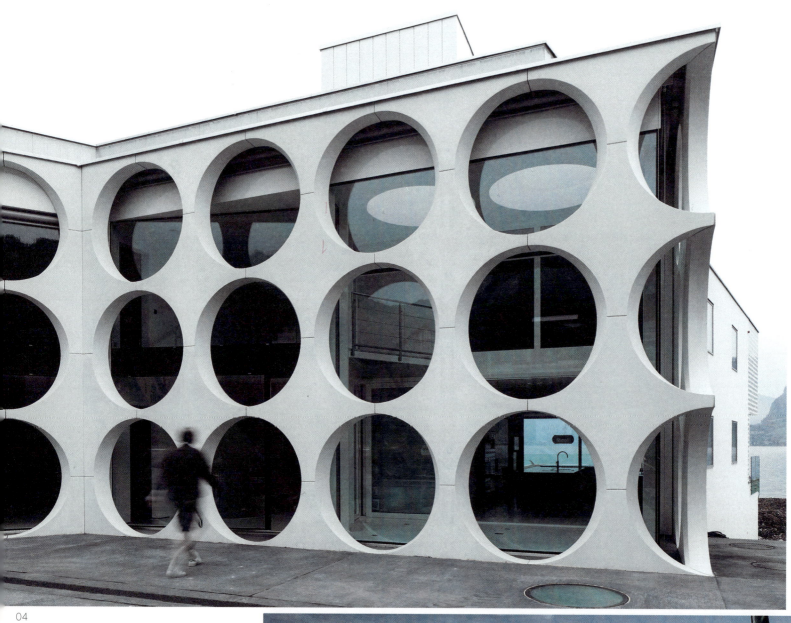

04

Beachlife~
Residential

Project~
O House
Lake Lucerne,
Switzerland

05

04—05~
Giant portholes dot the white façade made of prefab concrete elements.

06~
The O house has two main façades, the one saving the lake also features round shapes, but these consists of small glass elements, approximately 15 cm in diameter.

07~
Seated in a chaise in front of the fireplace, one has a great view of Lake Lucerne and, in the background, Mount Rigi and Bürgenstock.

Architects~
Will Alsop,
Sarah Featherstone,
Piers Gough

Client~
Jeremy Paxton

Completed~
To be completed

Website~
www.lowermillestate.com

Renderings by
CGI, Smoothe

Howels Mere, located in the Cotswolds of Gloucestershire, represents the third stage of property mogul Jeremy Paxton's Lower Mill Estate, a 450-acre development designed to include 140 houses that respond to their natural environment, many of which 'hover' over one of the estate's seven lakes. Each has an open-plan interior and windows that run the length of the façade and overlook the surrounding countryside. Eight have been designed by leading UK architects. Paxton, who is adamant that these eight fulfill the same criteria as the rest of the estate, wants them 'to fit within a certain footprint', 'to be built for a certain price' and 'to be environmentally responsible'. He says 'they have to grow from nature rather than just land on it'.
Resembling a tunnel segment, architect Will Alsop's design features a timber-clad arch that develops into a fully glazed winter garden. A sculptural, double-height, freestanding concrete structure divides the entrance and reception area from an otherwise open ground floor. The three bedrooms upstairs—'pods' suspended above the living space—are connected by a gallery. A one-lane swimming pool stretches along the eastern façade. Sarah Featherstone's façade for Orchid House, inspired by the camouflage of the bee orchid—here burnt into the timber, looks like a partly peeled orange. Made from veneer ribs and clad in timber shingles, the organic form seems eager to perch on any waterfront site. Living and dining wings fan out from a centrally positioned kitchen to generate an intimate courtyard with terraces, a gangway and a pontoon cascading forth like the petals of an orchid.
On the ground floor of Piers Gough's Watermark House, a boathouse and entrance hall are separated by a changing area. Architectural ribbons skirting a central core mark the exterior walls of the house, which spiral up in the opposite direction to the staircase indoors, overlapping and undulating to create open terraces. Inside, the double-width staircase curves round two floors to arrive at an 18-m-long rooftop 'infinity pool'.

01~
Elevations of Gough's Watermark House.

Front elevation

Side elevation

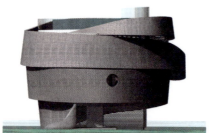
Rear elevation

Side elevation 2

Beachlife~
Residential

Landmark Houses Gloucestershire, UK

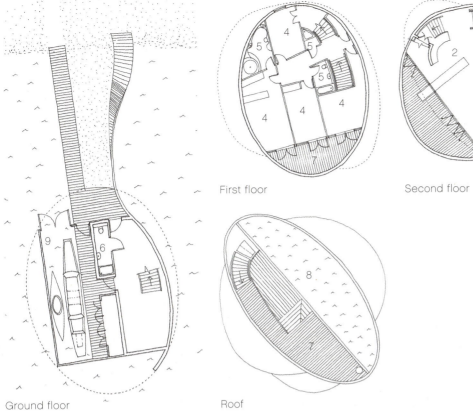

First floor

Second floor

Ground floor

Roof

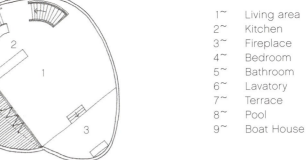

1~ Living area
2~ Kitchen
3~ Fireplace
4~ Bedroom
5~ Bathroom
6~ Lavatory
7~ Terrace
8~ Pool
9~ Boat House

02

Ground floor

First floor

Second floor

208 | 209

Beachlife~
Residential

Project~
Landmark Houses
Gloucestershire, UK

02~
Orchid House by Featherstone Associates.

03—04~
The Alsop House by Will Alsop.

Housing Block
Izola, Slovenia

Architect~
Ofis Arhitekti

Client~
Slovenia Housing Fund,
Community of Izola

Structural engineer~
Valid

Mechanical engineer~
Oves

Electrical engineer~
Winky

Construction~
Makro 5, Kraski Zidar

Total surface (m²)~
2294

Total cost (€)~
1,491,100

Completed~
2006

Website~
www.ofis-a.si

Photography by
Tomaz Gregoric

Beachlife~
Residential

A housing block atop a hill in Slovenia, with views of Izola Bay on one side and a mountainous landscape on the other, Ofis Arhitekti's design was realized after it won a competition organized by the Slovenia Housing Fund. Recognized for its economic, rational and functional advantages—including flexible floor plans and a good balance between gross and saleable surface areas—the design responded to a brief for attractive low-cost accommodation for young families. The apartment complexes, which were erected on two 60-x-28-m sites, contain 30 units of different types and sizes, from studio flats to three-bedroom apartments.

Although the rooms are small, they have been kept free of structural elements, leaving occupants with interiors that can be arranged in any number of ways. Projecting cheerfully from the façades are colourful geometric balconies, which extend the living area and provide a perfect outdoor vantage point—private, shady, airy and yet linked to the interior—for enjoying the surrounding vistas. Wide canvas awnings in a variety of bright colours give each dwelling a unique identity while providing protection from prying eyes and the Adriatic sun.

01~
Beehives served as inspiration for the design of Ofis's colourful apartment complex in Izola, Slovenia.

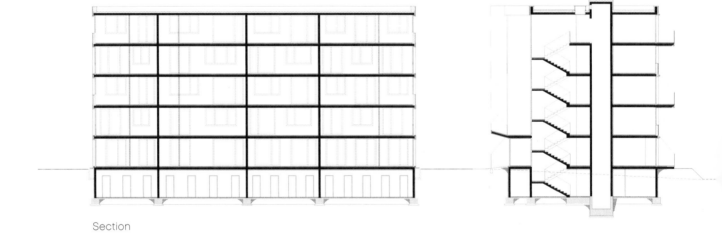

Section

Light*house
Aarhus, Denmark

Architects~
UNStudio,
3XN,
Gehl Architects

Clients~
Keops Development
K/S Frederiksbjerg
Ejendomme Arbejdernes
Andels Boligforening
Boligforeningen Ringgården

Site provider~
Municipality of Aarhus

Consulting engineer~
Grontmij | Carl Bro

Total floor area (m²)~
60,000

Estimated total cost (DKK)~
2 billion

Scheduled construction~
2008—2010

Website~
www.unstudio.com

Renderings by
UNStudio

Beachlife~
Residential

Two firms familiar with projects built on or near the water, Amsterdam's UNStudio and Danish architects 3XN joined forces to create the winning proposal for a waterfront housing competition for Aarhus, a city on the east coast of Denmark.

The brief asked for a residential complex, a quarter of which was to be reserved for non-profit-making rental units. The winning entry, Light*house, features an entirely new harbour promenade that offers a rich mix of cultural activities intended to serve a socially diverse community.

Challenged by a project divided into some 40,000 m² for housing and about 20,000 m² for commercial facilities, UNStudio and 3XN called on the services of Gehl Architects, experts in urban environments and an organization with comprehensive experience gathered through work on harbour environments from Australia and New Zealand to Norway and the USA. Involved in the Aarhus project from the beginning, Gehl ensures a vibrant, attractive and safe result, for both residents and visitors. Clearly marking the site will be a 140-m-high tower. Housing on either side of the tower will include 270 flats and 30 terraced houses. To create a unified image, the façades of all dwellings, whether rented or privately owned, are to be dissected by a series of white lines that refer to reflections of light on the water. The project has been designed to provide all residential units with sun from the south and a view to the north. In the words of UNStudio, the residents of Light*house will be able 'to live the view'.

01~
Clearly making the Light*house housing project visible from land, sea and air is a 140-m-high tower.

02~
Footbridges over the water connect the various parts of the residential development.

03~
Above the busy streets, a roof garden provides an area of relaxation.

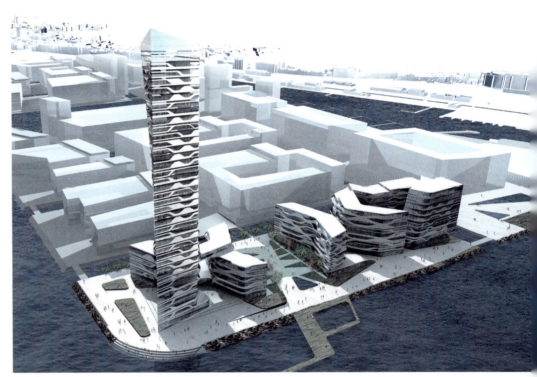
01

Periscope Houses
Rotterdam, the Netherlands

Architect~
Joke Vos architecten

Client~
Assink Vastgoed
Projectontwikkeling

Structural consultant~
Adviesburo Buizer

Building contractor~
Van Houwelingen Gorkum

Total floor area (m²)~
3035

Total cost (€)~
3,300,000

Completed~
October 2006

Website~
www.jokevos.nl

Photography by
Ger van der Vlugt

Rotterdam's Periscope Houses—a suitable name for homes that offer views in various directions—were realized in 2006. Situated at the edge of Waterwijk, one of the three development areas that make up a new urban district on the east side of Rotterdam called Nesselande, the compact dwellings—four clusters of three homes each—are completely surrounded by water. Each trio of homes is connected at the centre. The panelled aluminium volumes of the periscopes—shells that contain most of the living area—slice through a solid core of dark metallic bricks at angles to ensure that the balconies of all three units remain private. Framing the landscape like a sequence of picture postcards, fenestration is arranged within a grid of wooden panels. Like a three-dimensional jigsaw puzzle, the floor plan provides occupants with a flexible programme that can be organized in any number of ways.

The dwellings evidently belong to the same family yet display characteristic differences, such as entrance locations and balcony widths. On the first floor sliding doors open up the living room to a to a balcony with a view over the water. The ground floor continues outside from the private garage, where it becomes a waterside terrace. As an appropriate option for those living in a country that is partly built on water, Periscope Houses provides residents with docks for mooring small boats.

01~
Joke Vos architecten clad the buildings in durable, low-maintenance materials, including dark metallic bricks and aluminium panelling.

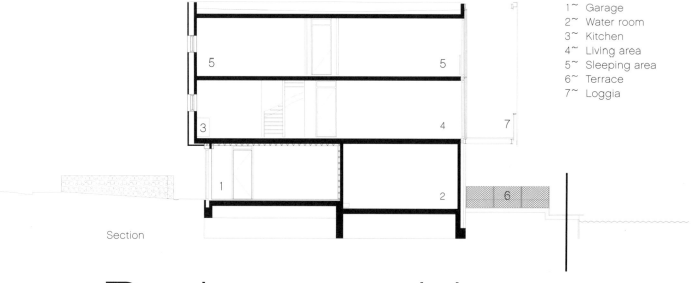

1~ Garage
2~ Water room
3~ Kitchen
4~ Living area
5~ Sleeping area
6~ Terrace
7~ Loggia

Section

Beachlife~
Residential

02

03

216 | 217

Beachlife~
Residential

Project~
Periscope Houses
Rotterdam,
the Netherlands

02~
During the summer, blinds made from western red cedar keep the houses cool.

03~
The living area on the first floor features a balcony overlooking the water.

04~
Surrounded by water, the 12 Periscope Houses have been built in clusters of three. True to their name, the houses offer occupants views in virtually all directions.

Floating Home
Berlin, Germany

Architect~
Gruentuch Ernst Architects

Client~
Wasserstadt Berlin

Total surface (m²)~
211

Completed~
Unrealized

Website~
www.gruentuchernst.de

Renderings by
Gruentuch Ernst Architects

Like vehicles whose wheels are submerged in the water, Gruentuch Ernst Architects' arched floating homes resemble modern caravans—more suited to soaking up views of the changing horizon in a harbour in Cannes or Nice than in Rummelsburg Bay, an inlet of Berlin's Spree River. Gruentuch Ernst's sleek design includes a domed glass ceiling and an exposed back. The highly polished, open-plan interiors of the upper level and the circular apertures of the 'cabin' level are comparable to those of a luxury yacht. Connected to the shore via a series of steps—joined in the middle by a small platform—the homes were designed to form urban clusters: floating neighbourhoods of up to eight units, a small enough number to maintain the privacy of individual residences. The winning concept of a competition launched by Wasserstadt Berlin, Gruentuch Ernst's floating home is just 7.5m wide. When not moored to the riverbank, the dwellings are capable of navigating all the city's waterways and locks. Residents who like the idea of holidaying at home will love living in a vessel that permits them to travel without the fear of leaving personal possessions behind.

01~
Gruentuch Ernst Architects' arched floating homes are not tied to one location—they can sail around the world.

02~
A few steps connect a small floating lawn to the back of the vessel.

03~
Interior of the floating home.

04~
An attractive location for mooring an attractive houseboat.

05~
The owner of a floating home has no trouble navigating a city's waterways.

01

02

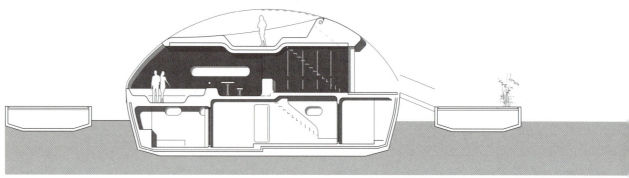
Section

Beachlife~
Residential

Architect~
Anthony Lau

Designed~
June 2007

Website~
www.tonylaudesign.com

Photography by
Jessica Lee

Global warming and its impending impact on the world as we know it are, in the words of environmental activist Al Gore, an 'inconvenient truth'. Coastal areas face the threat of inundation, and those hankering for seaside living may soon have only one option: housing that is literally 'on the water'. Planning for the inevitable, Anthony Lau designed Floating City—an aquatic form of urban expansion—for the Thames Estuary. Rather than constructing new-build offshore communities comprised of floating and stilt-supported architecture, Lau—keen to reduce energy costs in the production and maintenance of such housing—proposes the use of decommissioned ships and oil platforms to implement his design. Tied to the cultural heritage of the site, these resources would be a nautical reminder of the city's history and affinity with the water. The inventive architecture in Lau's proposal would give the 700 large vessels scrapped every year a secondary function. Converted ships could accommodate terraced housing or multistorey apartment complexes by utilizing the exiting container-stacking grid. Interconnected by walkways, Lau's self-sufficient floating units harness renewable energy sources (wind, solar, tidal) and rely to some extent on food grown on neighbouring platforms. In terms of entertainment, the mobile infrastructure has room for floating sports stadiums and spaces for special events like weekend markets. Not exclusive to the UK, this strategy for creating self-sufficient floating communities by reusing ships and marine structures is also suitable for island nations such as the Maldives, which, with over 80 per cent of its 1200 islands 1 m above sea level, could be inhabitable within 100 years.

02

01

Beachlife~
Residential

Flooded Future 2050
Thames Estuary, UK

01~
Architect Anthony Lau sees a future in which decommissioned ships are converted into floating arks on the mudflats of the Thames Estuary.

02~
Semi-submersible rigs can be towed and sunk into position.

Converting decommissioned ships.

03~
A decommissioned ship used as floating platform.

04~
Model of Floating City 2050.

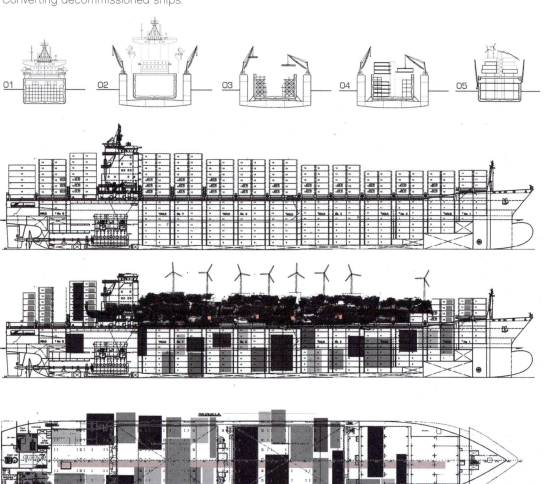

Beachlife~
Residential

Project~
Flooded Future 2050
Thames Estuary, UK

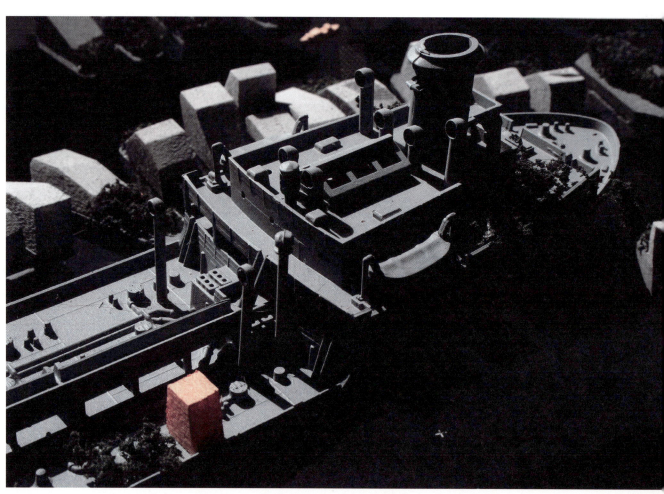

03

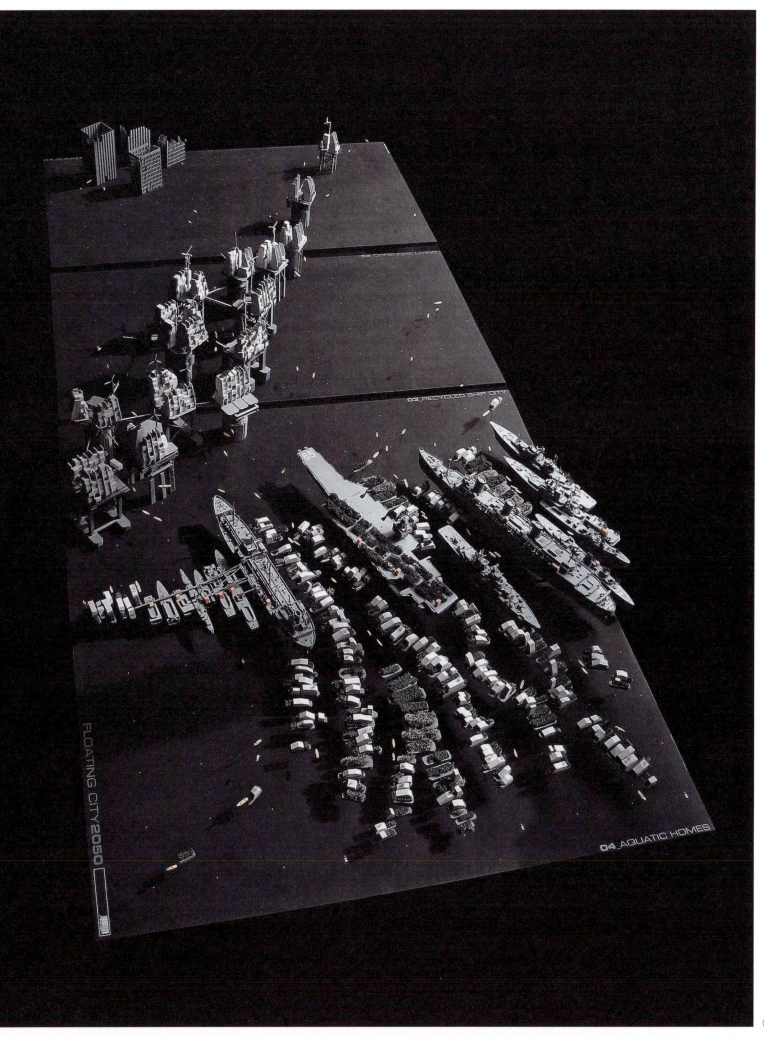

05

Beachlife~
Residential

Project~
Flooded Future 2050
Thames Estuary, UK

06

05~
Both terrace-type housing and multistorey apartments can be created by reusing existing container-stacking grids.

06~
The proposed city depends on wind-, solar- and tidal-powered energy.

07~
In Lau's floating city, oil rigs become high-rises.

08~
Planted terraces and private gardens are created within the oil-platform housing.

09~
Roads are water routes, and cars are replaced by boats.

07

08

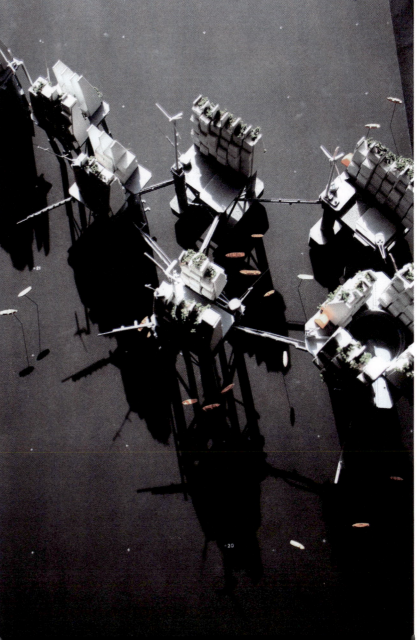
09

Seaside Apartment
Knokke, Belgium

Designer~
Doorzon Interior Architects

Manufacturers~
Obumex,
Lucas De Smedt,
Van Den Weghe,
Vera Vermeersch

Total floor area (m²)~
128

Duration of construction~
1 year

Completed~
March 2007

Website~
www.doorzon.be

Photography by
Frederik Vercruysse

Part of a residential development in Knokke, the seaside apartment designed by Doorzon Interior Architects has breathed new life into a stretch of the Belgian coast. Keeping in mind the high demands of the beachfront-property owners, which include enough room to welcome the occasional guest, the designers went to work. The apartment has two major zones: a living area and a private area. A pristine white marble floor in the living area reflects both light and the ever-changing colours of the North Sea. An open-plan kitchen can be separated from the living room by closing a large cabinet door, concealing appliances and the bright blue colour of the kitchen. The marble floor extends into the hallway and towards the guest room, where visitors find a woollen carpet with a marble motif. The private area, which accommodates bedroom and bathroom, is at one end of a corridor lined with built-in ebony cupboards. Marble flooring adds a touch of luxury to the bathroom as well, completing the picture.

01~
In Knokke, guest rooms in an apartment designed by Doorzon feature portholes as windows, an appropriate choice considering the view.

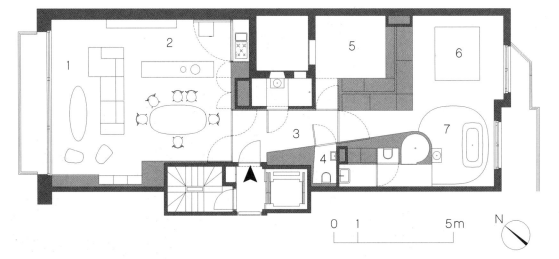

Floor plan

1~ Living area
2~ Kitchen
3~ Hallway
4~ Lavatory
5~ Guest room
6~ Bedroom
7~ Bathroom

Beachlife~
Residential

03

02

228 | 229

Beachlife~
Residential

Project~
Seaside Apartment
Knokke, Belgium

04

02~
The apartment complex lies on the coast of Belgium. Opening the large sliding doors between living room and balcony draws the sea breeze into the dwelling.

03~
A sliding door opens to reveal bookshelves (left) or a flatscreen TV (right).

04~
A large blue cabinet door separates the living area from the kitchen. Leaving the door open merges the two rooms into a single space.

05~
Th lavatory is covered with tactiles, handmade tiles by Koninklijke Tichelaar, Makkum.

06~
In the master bedroom, blue silk curtains open to reveal a marble-floored bathroom.

07~
The 'porthole and marble' theme continues in the bathroom adjacent to the guest room.

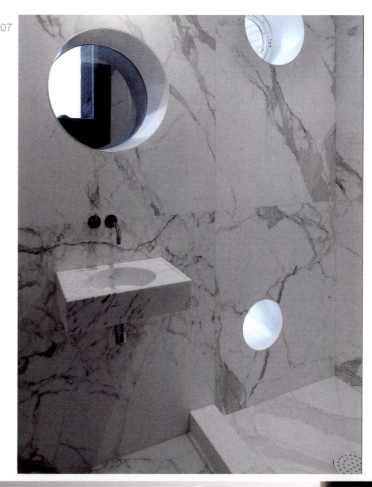

Architect~
Markus Wikar

Website~
www.markuswikar.com

Renderings by
Markus Wikar

Inspired by childhood summers spent on lakes in Finland—and driven by a desire to escape his inner-city apartment—Markus Wikar designed a floating house, a type of dwelling that is becoming more and more popular as cities struggle to accommodate rising populations. A fusion of city and country living, Wikar's houseboat aims to give urbanites the best of both worlds. Nothing at all like the fume-filled concrete blocks currently on offer, the house provides occupants with direct access to the water, transforming the front porch into an ice-skating rink during the winter months and a lake for kayaking in the summer. Prefabricated elements can be transported on a lorry and lifted onto concrete pontoons on site. Floating on the water, a row of these buildings—with their larch-slatted exterior walls supported by steel frames—presents a pleasingly uniform appearance. Larch, renowned for its resistance to the elements, weathers to a gentle grey in the course of time. Wikar has left his plain white interiors blank, to be customized by the occupants' choice of furniture and textiles. Designed to outlive both the interior décor and the structure itself, the concrete pontoons can be anchored to the seabed in a variety of ways, from chains to elastic mooring systems.

01~
Steel-framed exterior walls are clad in larch, a highly weather-resistant timber that requires very little maintenance.

02~
The interior can be customized to meet individual specifications. Markus Wikar's basic white space is a neutral envelope meant to be enlivened by splashes of colour from furniture, textiles and the occupants themselves.

03~
Ideally, the house should be built in an area with the infrastructure needed to connect it to communal sewerage and heating systems. The floating house can also be equipped, however, with a septic tank and a heat pump.

1~ Living area
2~ Dining area
3~ Kitchen
4~ Bedroom
5~ Bathroom
6~ Sauna

Ground floor

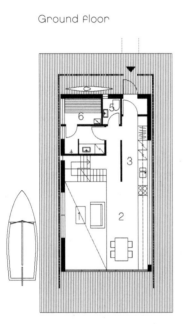

First floor

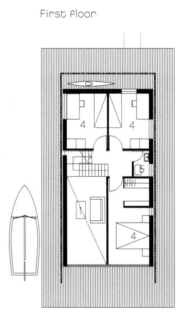

Roof terrace

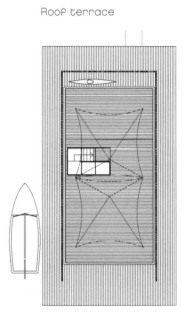

Beachlife~
Residential

Floating House Concept

Designers~
IUAV students

Organization~
Cibic Workshop

Duration of construction~
3 weeks

Completed~
July 2007

Website~
www.cibicworkshop.com

Photography by
Tommaso Corá

Led by Italian design studio Cibic&Partners, in the summer of 2007 students from the Architecture University Institute of Venice (IUAV) were asked to create a sustainable settlement in the inland regions of Jesolo Lagoon, near Venice. The community was to be located on a 5-km-long peninsula in an area known for its fishing activities. Participants were asked to develop ideas for a site that would remain inviting all year round, an oasis outside the city promoting a harmonious existence with nature, where people would want to live off the land, work together and have fun. The micro-economies in the students' proposals—designed to appeal to both nature-loving families and singles—included opportunities for breeding animals and growing fruit and vegetables. The brief asked for a focus on green areas and landscaping and for serious consideration of the aesthetics of each architectural object introduced into a plan. With only three weeks to fine-tune their proposals, the 25 groups of IUAV students presented solutions complete with dwellings, high-tech tents, living greenhouses, photovoltaic panels, aeolic generators, underground cisterns and solar panels. Proof that life outdoors does not limit the happy camper to bathing in the lake by the light of the moon.

01~
Waterways in the lagoon lend access to the land.

02~
Structures for ecotourism on a peninsula in the Jesolo Lagoon. Wooden dwellings built on piles offer great observation points for animal- and bird-watching.

01

Beachlife~
Residential

Living in Nature
Jesolo Lagoon, Italy

234 | 235

Beachlife~
Residential

Project~
Living in Nature
Jesolo Lagoon, Italy

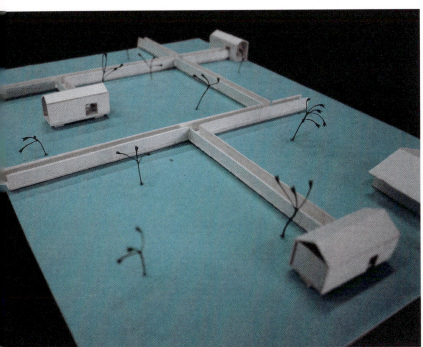

06

03—05~
All structures are made from natural materials; the result is a communal park where artists and others can live and work surrounded by nature.

06—08~
The structures proposed do not compromise the ecosystem of the region. The objective is to allow and support the environmentally conscious tourist to tiptoe into nature.

07

08

Architect~
Waterstudio.NL

Client~
BAM

Consultant~
DHV

Total cost (€)~
3 million

Completed~
Under construction

Website~
www.waterstudio.nl

Renderings by
Waterstudio.NL,
BAM

Beachlife~
Residential

A Dutch firm that specializes in architecture and urbanism—projects related to living, working and playing on the water—Waterstudio.NL is in the process of realizing a floating apartment complex in IJburg, a developing neighbourhood not far from Amsterdam. The architects' Stilt Houses utilize a seemingly uninhabitable piece of property. Appearing to wade into the water, the dwellings perch atop a series of stilts, as their name suggests, surrounded partly by the IJ Lake and partly by land. An economical use of space, the design includes an area underneath the structures which is ideal for mooring boats and enjoying the scenery from terraces located here. Above this space, extending from glazed walls that cover the front of the apartments, large balconies further ensure a true appreciation of the waterfront panorama. Square in shape and split into two levels, the housing will remain dry even when land-anchored neighbours face the danger of flooding.

01~
Terraces underneath the Stilt Houses are perfect for mooring boats.

02—03~
In the event of flooding, only the terraces at the bases of Waterstudio's Stilt Houses would be submerged. The houses themselves have been designed to remain dry.

01

Stilt Houses IJburg, the Netherlands

02

03

Architect~
Javier Artadi

Structural engineer~
Jorge Indacochea

Total surface (m²)~
280

Completed~
January 2006

Website~
www.javierartadi.com

Photography by
Alexander Kornhuber

Located on a beachfront site 100 km south of Lima, architect Javier Artadi's Las Arenas Beach House resembles a remodelled shipping container. Deliberately suspended over the lawn to suggest a sense of weightlessness, the structure rests on a dark-grey terrazzo plinth and apparently hovers above the landscape. Spread throughout the entrance level are a living room, dining room, kitchen, laundry room, terrace and pool. Four bedrooms remain shielded from the Peruvian heat in the basement. Artadi created interesting visual effects—and simultaneously coped with the bright sunlight—by strategically cutting certain faces of the volume, exposing the interior and making a smooth transition between indoor and outdoor spaces. People inside the house have a clear view of the terrace, the pool and, by extension, the horizon, while those enjoying the pool can float on their backs and gaze at the stars. The many interior sightlines are another pleasant result of Artadi's clever design. Open on all sides, the residence is rarely plagued by rainstorms, as this seaside area is one of the driest spots on earth.

01~
Javier Artadi created a smooth transition between the interior of the beach house and its surroundings by opening up the white concrete boxes that form the basis of his design.

02~
The pool offers a view of the Pacific.

1~ Living room
2~ Dining room
3~ Kitchen
4~ TV room
5~ Bedroom
6~ Bathroom
7~ Lavatory
8~ Laundry room
9~ Storage
10~ Pool
11~ Terrace

01

Las Arenas Beach House Lima, Peru

Beachlife~
Residential

Underground level

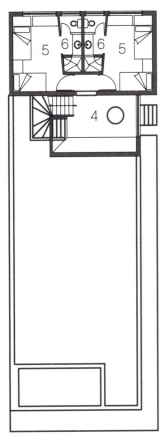

Terrace level

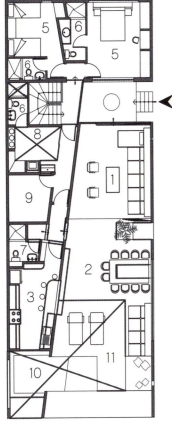

Beachlife~
Products

Products

Designer~
Lianne van Genugten

Materials~
Polypropylene,
flexible solar cells,
aluminium

Dimensions~
250 x 300 cm
(other sizes available
on request)

Completed prototype~
2007

Website~
www.liannevangenugten.nl

Photography by
Marieke van Esch

A product normally redundant after dusk, Lianne van Genugten's SunShade collects energy during the day—by means of flexible solar cells embedded in the shade—and becomes an outdoor lamp by night. Automated by sensors, the parasol opens and closes like a mechanized flower as it reacts to the presence and absence of sunlight. When its white panels fold inwards, the result is a giant illuminated lampshade. Made to order, Sunshade is perfect for quiet sunny days and long evenings on the beach.

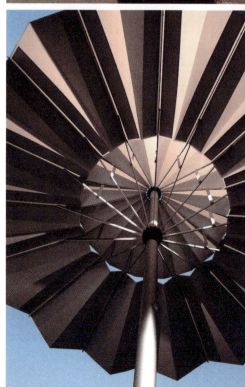

SunShade

Designer~
Jan Melis

Manufacturer~
Symo/Sywawa

Material~
Polyethylene

Dimensions~
45 x 45 x 45 cm

Colours~
White, lime green, taupe

Completed~
2007

Websites~
www.symo.be
www.sywawa.com

Photography by Symo

An alternative to sinking your parasol in the sand—only to watch helplessly, minutes later, as the wind wrenches it out and sends it sailing towards the sea—Cube is a waterside necessity. Designed by Jan Melis for Sywawa—a branch of Symo, a Belgian manufacturer of parasols and umbrellas—Cube draws all eyes to the base of your sunshade. A multifunctional design, the hollow square not only holds your parasol in place, but also functions as a table or handy pouf (a made-to-fit cushion adds extra comfort to the seat). Light and easy to transport, Cube can be filled with water or sand for increased stability.

Cube

Canasta

Designer~
Patricia Urquiola

Manufacturer~
B&B Italia

Materials~
Aluminium, steel, polyethylene, ceramic tile, water-repellent fabric

Completed~
2007

Website~
www.bebitalia.com

Photography by
B&B Italia

Traditional and contemporary production techniques are interwoven in Patricia Urquiola's Canasta collection. (Canasta is the Spanish word for 'basket'.) Taking a cue from objects made of Viennese straw, B&B Italia had strong strips of polyethylene woven by hand by skilled craftsmen in the Philippines. Polyethylene is a lightweight material that makes this line of outdoor furniture exceptionally sturdy and durable. Wrapped in a lattice of interwoven bands that create an openwork surface punctured with holes for good ventilation, the diversely formed pieces of the collection share a common aesthetic. Seating—including large bowl-shaped chairs made extra comfy with an assortment of patterned cushions, sunbeds with reclining backrests, and theatrical thrones with raised backs that curve round to conceal the occupant—is complemented by a choice of tables, with bases of varnished steel and ceramic-tiled tops. Patterns on the cushions are repeated in these tiled surfaces, ensuring a harmonious outdoor ensemble that can be configured in any number of ways.

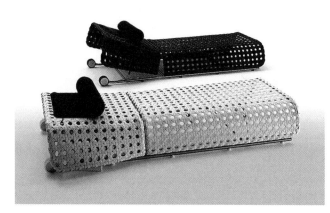

Designer~
Sander Bokkinga / bok.

Materials~
Plywood, wood, steel

Dimensions~
3 x 25 x 50 cm

Colours~
White, green, yellow

Completed~
2007

Website~
www.sanderbokkinga.nl

Photography by
Sander Bokkinga

Sander Bokkinga—the man behind bok—knows that building moat-encircled castles on the beach can be quite a labour-intensive activity. An adaptation of an existing tool, the bok.shovelseat is Bokkinga's reinterpretation of the garden spade. The energetic holidaymaker can use the shovel to build a mighty fortress before plunging it into the sand, where it becomes a backrest to support the weary architect. Launched at Milan's Salone del Mobile in 2007, the shovel-cum-chair is a prime example of 'function follows form'. Also included in Bokkinga's collection of furniture that doubles as tools is the clever bok.pitchforkchair.

bok.shovelseat

Designers~
GAEAforms/
Pinar Yar,
Tugrul Gövsa

Manufacturer~
Gövsa Composites

Materials~
Composite shell,
polyurethane,
MDF and more

Colours~
White, black, green,
purple, navy, dark brown,
red, turquoise, sand

Completed~
2008

Website~
www.gaeaforms.com

Photography by
GAEAforms

Envision a parade of pieces belonging to GAEAforms' Step collection arranged in a line along the coast: the image is one of a new generation of animals waiting to board Noah's ark. Intrigued by lines, proportions and materials, the designers took a playful approach to the creation of a family of furniture composed of unique pieces—each with its own story—united by similar characteristics. Sharing the same sleek skin are an ergonomically designed chair, stool, ottoman, bench and small workstation. Suitable for both indoor and outdoor use, and available in a range of vivid colours, GAEAforms' collection of fluidly formed furniture, with its sculptural aesthetic, is a giant step above the ordinary.

Step

Designers~
Students of the
HfG-Karlsruhe,
Germany

Design team~
Laura Bernhardt,
Benedikt Achatz,
Tom Förderer,
Bastian Goecke,
Johannes Marmon,
Johannes Müller,
Kilian Schindler,
Martin Sprekelsen,
Moritz Willborn

Supervisors~
Werner Aisslinger,
Stefan Legner

Completed~
April 2004

Websites~
www.quicnic.de
www.benedikt-achatz.com

Photography by
Students of the
HfG-Karlsruhe

Chairs posing as tree trunks, grass underfoot and picnic baskets scattered throughout: the only authentic picnic accompaniment missing from Quicnic is a swarm of flies. At the Salone del Mobile in Milan, the designers of this futuristic concept—students from HfG-Karlsruhe, a school in Germany—presented several objects that together form 'a picnic fast-food restaurant'.

Using the objects separately is an equally logical option. Grey-and-white cylinders can be slotted together to form clusters that invite users to socialize. Multifunctional, these objects form seats that double as backrests and tables that double as seats.

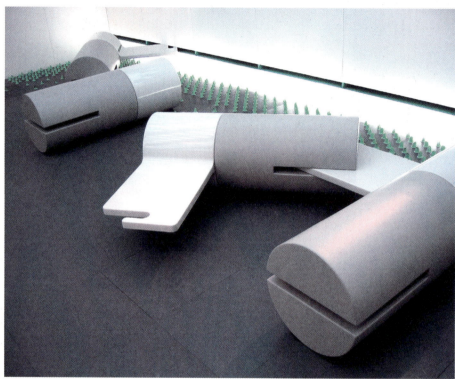

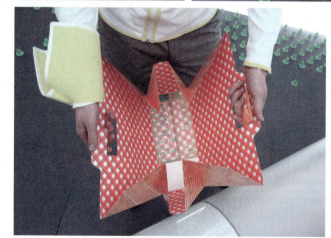

Quicnic

Beachlife~
Products

Designer~
Dirk Wynants

Manufacturer~
Extremis

Material~
Rotation-moulded polyethylene

Completed~
2006

Website~
www.extremis.be

Photography by Extremis

Whether used separately or combined, these multifunctional objects create a cosy campfire atmosphere. The saddle-shaped Bronco, which provides seating, features a leather strap that serves as a cup holder—no more burying your drink halfway in the sand to keep it from tipping over. Realizing that seven triangular Broncos form a perfect circle, designer Dirk Wynants was inspired to create Corral-cum-C'upsidedown, which can be used either as a matching table (Corral) or a striking pendant lamp (C'upsidedown). A colour filter used with any or all of these objects changes standard white light into whatever shade you have in mind. Generate an environment to fit the occasion.

Bronco, Corral, C'upsidedown

Designers~
The Nomad Concept, L'Anverre

Manufacturer~
The Nomad Concept

Materials~
Aluminium, polyester

Colours~
White, ecru, anthracite, red, terracotta

Surface~
10 m² (other sizes available as well)

Completed~
2005

Website~
www.nomadconcept.com

Photography by
L'Anverre

Pinched in the centre and drawn up to form a peak, Umbella looks like the head of a lily flipped upside down. When used on the beach, its pointy petals cast a sprightly shadow on the sand. Designed by 'sail sculpture specialists' The Nomad Concept and art collective L'Anverre, the asymmetric Umbella leans into the sun, soaking up its rays. Inspired by Japan's annual Sakura Festival, which draws crowds of people who picnic beneath an illuminated canopy of cherry blossoms, the parasol is made from two non-concentric circles of high-tech polyester. Metal components are aluminium. Lightweight and functional, Umbella has a patented system for opening and closing the canopy, making the product quick and easy to set up and store after use.

Umbella

Designer~
Nacho Carbonell Ivars

Manufacturer~
Nacho Carbonell

Materials~
Sand, rubber

Dimensions~
Each bench is made to order

Completed~
February 2007

Website~
www.nachocarbonell.com

Photography by
Jose van Riele,
Lilian van Rooij

At first glance, Nacho Carbonell Ivars' battered, sagging sofa looks as though it's reached the end of the line. In fact, the apparently dilapidated seat pictured here is straight off the production line, and Carbonell calls it an 'outdoor bench'. Addressing the frustration of children worldwide who see their architectural masterpieces washed away in a single swell of the sea, he created Dream of Sand, a malleable volume of sand held together by a rubber coating. Pushed, patted and pulled into shape, the sofa can be moulded to form an extension of an existing structure, given the characteristics of its immediate envi-ronment, or used as a stand-alone seating solution. Dream of Sand remains flexible without compromising the user's comfort. The bench is perfect for a day of basking in the sun—without having to endure the discomfort of sand in every crevice!

Dream of Sand

Designer~
Wiel Arets

Manufacturer~
Gutzz

Materials~
Polyethylene, Lycra

Dimensions~
190 x 69 cm

Colours~
Black, white

Completed~
2007

Websites~
www.wielarets.nl
www.gutzz.com

Photography by
Peter Heesakkers/Gutzz

Beachlife~
Products

The first piece of outdoor furniture to be included in the Gutzz collection of art objects, the B'kini Chair has no 'right side up'. Flip it over, lie with head down and feet up, try it the other way round—anything goes. Architect Wiel Arets designed the multifunctional lounge chair, which Gutzz introduced at Maison&Objet Paris. Curvy side up, B'kini invites you to sit, read, chat, scan the crowd in and around the pool.

The long slope on the opposite side is great for snoozing in the sun while working on that perfect tan. Arets designed the ergonomic chair to support and stretch the back, relieving spinal pressure and enhancing relaxation. Made from polyethylene, B'kini is available in either black or white. Added comfort comes in the form of a matching, hand-knotted Lycra cushion.

B'kini Chair

Designer~
Danny Fang

Manufacturer~
Kian

Materials~
Aluminium,
polyethylene wicker

Dimensions~
Papa Chair:
72 x 88 x 83 cm
Mama Chair:
64 x 73 x 72 cm
Child 1:
55 x 60 x 26 cm
Child 2:
44 x 48 x 24 cm

Completed~
2007

Website~
www.fangstudio.com

Photography by
Fang Studio

Stowaways. Neatly stacked inside Dang Fang's Matryoshka Chair, six forms come together to create a set of chairs and stools. A collection of lightweight outdoor furniture fabricated from aluminium and polyethylene wicker, Fang's furniture is inspired by traditional Russian matryoshka dolls. Nicknamed by Fang—Papa Chair, Mama Chair, Child 1 and Child 2—the seating objects, like the dolls, represent people: all similar, but different in either size or shape. The archetypical family. While Papa Chair plays the role of protector, Mama Chair keeps the children safe within her bosom.

Matryoshka Chair

Designer~
PS Lab/Pepijn Smit

Material~
PVC

Dimensions~
85 x 70 x 80 cm

Colours~
Red, white, blue, black and silver

Completed~
2006

Website~
www.pslab.nl

Photography by
PS Lab

Objects normally seen bobbing up and down on the waves, like plump swimmers out of their depth, buoys provided PS Lab with the bright idea that led to Chairbag. A bulbous, slouching form bent up to create a triangular backrest, the product is, according to the designers, a cross between a beanbag and an easy chair. Inflatable and waterproof, with a practical handle on top for easy transport, this PVC blob is the perfect beach accessory. Available in an assortment of bold colours, Chairbag is a handy marker, in or out of the water.

Chairbag

Designer~
oneQ/Jan Willem Marijnissen

Manufacturer~
oneQ

Materials~
Powder-coated galvanized steel, stainless steel, wood

Dimensions~
Mini:
44 x 44 x 44 cm
Standard:
92 x 44 x 44 cm
Large:
110 x 44 x 44 cm

Completed~
2007

Website~
www.one-q.com

Photography by
Hans Oostrum fotografie

In future, holidaymakers should think twice before accusing their partners of having 'packed everything but the kitchen sink'. Why? Because Dutch designer Jan Willem Marijnissen's oneQ barbeque removes the 'but' from that allegation. Launched in the spring of 2007, Marijnissen's modular cooking system is set to revolutionize outdoor cooking. The customer can design a personal kitchen (large, standard or mini) by selecting items from a wide range of cooking appliances and accessories including grills (gas or charcoal), wok burner, teppanyaki plate, wooden tables and cutting board, sink and wine cooler. A minimalist design based on several small, square tables, oneQ can be kept simple for intimate barbecues or extended to form a fully functional kitchen for larger gatherings.

oneQ

Designer~
Marcel Wanders

Manufacturer~
SLIDE

Material~
Polyethylene

Dimensions~
Chubby:
130 x 120 x 56 cm
Chubby Low:
85 x 75 x 30 cm

Colours~
Green, red, grey, white

Weight~
25 kg

Completed~
2007

Website~
www.marcelwanders.com

Photography by
Marcel Wanders Studio

Beachlife~
Products

Chubby

Chubby, the love child of Marcel Wanders and SLIDE, is a remake of the Dutch designer's limited-edition Crochet Chair, which featured white crocheted flowers sewn together and stiffened with epoxy resin. Chubby, with its roto-moulded polyethylene shell, is a more affordable option aimed at the general public. Although lacking the intricate detail of fine needlework, Chubby—available in an assortment of colours—has all the dynamism of its older sibling. Thanks to a bold form and resilient structure, the chair is destined to become a favourite at get-togethers both indoors and out. An addition to the family, Chubby Low, is a curvaceous pouf shaped like a smooth pebble lying on the beach at low tide.

Designer~
Benedikt Achatz

Material~
Powder-coated steel

Dimensions~
Table: 820 x 700 x 530 cm
Rack: 860 x 900 x 530 cm

Completed~
2004

Website~
www.benedikt-achatz.com

Photography by
Dennis Orel

Marked by pebbles, windbreaks or lines drawn in the sand, many beaches turn into a landscape of micro living rooms during the summer months. To facilitate the transport of these temporal environments from home to seaside, designer Benedikt Achatz has developed a range of multifunctional products that put an end to picnics served with an accompaniment of sand and towels covered in a layer of grit. Achatz's basic+ folding table, which can be conveniently stowed away when not in use, includes a slatted top that can be pulled up to create a handy drying rack. Adjustable in height, the powder-coated steel rack can accommodate big beach towels (at full height) along with the skimpiest bikini.

Beachlife~
Products

basic+

Designers~
GAEAforms: Pinar Yar, Tugrul Govsa

Manufacturer~
GOVSA Composites

Materials~
Composites, Dacron

Dimensions~
260 x 115 x 20 cm

Colours~
White, black, green, purple, navy blue, dark brown, red, turquoise, sand

Completed~
2007

Website~
www.gaeforms.com

Photography by GAEAforms

Inspired by nature, Leaf is the world's first ergonomically designed hammock. Like all products manufactured by Turkish furniture brand GAEAforms, Leaf can be used both indoors and out. The concept behind the design targets potential users with busy schedules—people looking for ways to live a well-balanced life.

The hammock's injection-moulded composite shell provides maximum flexibility. A macramé field, bordered by this sturdy frame, features a distinctive type of Persian knotting in which all cords (each 3 mm in diameter) are tied to the shell individually, allowing them to be removed and replaced with new cords, one by one, if necessary. Both the composite material used for the frame and the Dacron cord are completely weatherproof and UV resistant. Tied between two palm trees, Leaf offers both luxury and relaxation—the perfect place for enjoying a day at the beach.

Leaf Hammock

Designer~
David Olschewski

Manufacturer~
David Olschewski

Materials~
Acrylic, steel, PVC

Dimensions~
47 x 54 x 55 cm

Completed~
2006

Website~
www.davidolschewski.de

Photography by
Miriam Holz

Beachlife~
Products

Sink or swim. Finding a secondary function for inflatable armbands that are of little use out of water, David Olschewski used eight water wings to create a cushioned stool. Afloat on dry land, the inflatable devices—resting on transparent acrylic-resin legs—appear to be suspended in midair. Intrinsically linked through function, although used in different contexts and playing different roles, water wings and stools are both sources of support. Were Olschewski's Schwimmfluegelhocker to be raised a couple of metres higher, the seat would make a perfect lookout for lifeguards—cushioned, highly visible and complete with an extra supply of swimming aids.

Schwimm-fluegelhocker

Designer~
Max Lamb

Manufacturer~
Max Lamb

Materials~
Pewter

Dimensions~
40 x 40 x 40 cm

Completed~
2006

Website~
www.maxlamb.org

Photography by
Jane Lamb,
Max Lamb

On Cornwall's southern coast, a nice combination of traditional and unconventional materials and methods led to Max Lamb's Pewter Stool. A project realized while the designer was studying for a master's degree in product design at London's RCA, the stool, unequivocally strong, appears as delicate as the sand used to mould it. Swapping bucket and spade for molten pewter and human hands, Lamb adopted a primitive technique, sculpting a sand mould directly into the surface of the beach and pouring liquid pewter from his mum's old saucepan into the mould.
No secondary work required: once the material had cooled, he dug away the sand to reveal the finished product, a stool with a smoothly fluid seat and the granular texture of sand imprinted on legs and underside.

Pewter Stool

Designer~
Nils Holger Moormann

Manufacturer~
Aicher Holzhausbau

Dimensions~
386 x 110 x 650 cm

Materials~
Steel, acrylic fabric, larch, birch plywood, solid spruce, Plexiglas

Completed~
2006

Website~
www.moormann.de

Photography by
Jäger & Jäger

This sculptural garden object—an open invitation to enjoy the outdoors—is the work of Nils Holger Moormann, who drew inspiration from Walden, a book in which American author and philosopher Henry David Thoreau describes the two years he spent in a cabin in the woods communing with nature. For the green thumbs among us, Moormann's Walden offers a broad gamut of storage possibilities for garden tools such as shovel, rake and wheelbarrow. For those more inclined to sit back and enjoy the garden while others do the work, Walden offers a cosy nook for dining 'out' and an upper level with a view of clouds floating by or stars twinkling at night. An extendible grill promises to make the evening hours even more pleasant.

01~
A small seating area in the middle of the object offers a cosy retreat for two.

02~
A bed on the upper level makes a night of stargazing much more comfortable.

03~
Walden offers a place for every gardening tool imaginable and, when assembled in the right location, great views of splendid surroundings.

02~
A small dwelling containing an even smaller dwelling: Moormann tucked a birdhouse into a tiny niche.

Walden

01

02

03

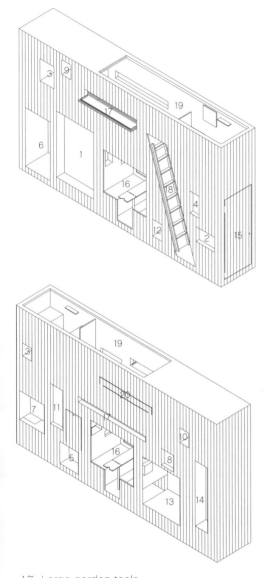

1~ Large garden tools
2~ Small garden tools
3~ Flower pot
4~ Garden shears
5~ Garden hose
6~ Garden hose
7~ Watering can
8~ Dust pan and brush
9~ Bird seeds
10~ Bird house
11~ Beer glasses
12~ Petroleum lamp
13~ Grill
14~ Fire wood
15~ Fire wood
16~ Sitting area
17~ Sunblind
18~ Ladder
19~ Upper level with bed
20~ Upper level window

Designer~
Höweler + Yoon Architecture

Material~
Polypropylene

Dimensions~
Various

Completed~
2006

Website~
www.hyarchitecture.com

Photography by
Höweler + Yoon Architecture

Thin polypropylene sheets that have been heat-formed over wooden moulds are transformed into a continuously curving transparent ribbon to create Höweler + Yoon's Loop Chair. Twisting and turning, the undulating plane closes in on itself to form a seat. The material used to make this flexible rocking chair has an inherent ductility and a high resistance to fatigue, both of which allow the chair's open profiles to support the weight of the body and conform precisely to the user's shape. Thanks to the lightness and delicacy of the architectural structure, sitting on a Loop feels like floating on air.

Loop Chairs

Designer~
José A. Gandia

Manufacturer~
Gandia Blasco

Materials~
Anodized aluminium, polyurethane foam, synthetic canvas

Dimensions~
Uno al Fresco:
90 x 90 x 200 cm
Tres al Fresco:
200 x 120 x 200 cm

Completed~
2007

Website~
www.gandiablasco.com

Photography by
Gandia Blasco

Out of sight, relaxing in the sun, the beachgoer lounging on Gandia Blasco's Uno al Fresco or Tres al Fresco occupies a personal spot at the water's edge. The Al Fresco collection boasts anodized-aluminium frames covered in synthetic canvas. In terms of form, the pieces of outdoor furniture, which shield the user from gusty side winds and searing heat, resemble old-fashioned changing booths. Available in two sizes, Al Fresco caters to the lone bather as well as to cosy gatherings. The design can be seen as an outdoor living room whose TV and remote control have been replaced by scenic views and bottles of tanning cream. Weather permitting, the sides of the structures—each side is a separate panel—can be adjusted to create a more or less open structure. When they catch the breeze, these panels billow like the sails of a ship.

Al Fresco

Designer~
Arne Quinze

Manufacturer~
Quinze & Milan

Material~
Upholstered UV foam

Colours~
Custom colours available

Completed~
2006

Website~
www.quinzeandmilan.tv

Photography by
Thierry Van Dort

Working alfresco? For those who find the transition between home and office difficult to define, Quinze & Milan has the perfect solution. Reinterpreting the traditional aesthetics of office furniture, the manufacturer's By the Pool collection consists of low upholstered chairs and ottomans realized in lightweight, water-repellent materials—perfect for the beach. Add a couple of Quinze & Milan's matching mesh screens to re-create the seclusion of the office cubicle in the warmth of the sun. Ideal for life outside the corporate bubble, the furniture is available in a wide range of colours. How about magenta? Or a stripy orange to go with that sexy bikini?

Beachlife~
Products

By the Pool

Designer~
Christophe Pillet

Manufacturer~
Tacchini

Materials~
Birch, steel (nickel-plated, satin finish), padding

Dimensions~
139 x 110 x 68 cm

Completed~
2006

Website~
www.christophepillet.com

Photography by
Marco Covi

Sinuously curved like a curled section of fencing, Christophe Pillet's South-Beach chair envelops the user within the sanctum of its slatted structure. A bulbous backrest tapers downward, forming a rather mysterious silhouette when viewed from the side. Designed for Italian manufacturer Tacchini, SouthBeach is made from solid strips of birch that are interconnected by nickel-plated bands of steel with a satin finish. Seat and headrest feature multi-layered birch and padding. The birch is available with a bleached finish, as well as painted either black or white.

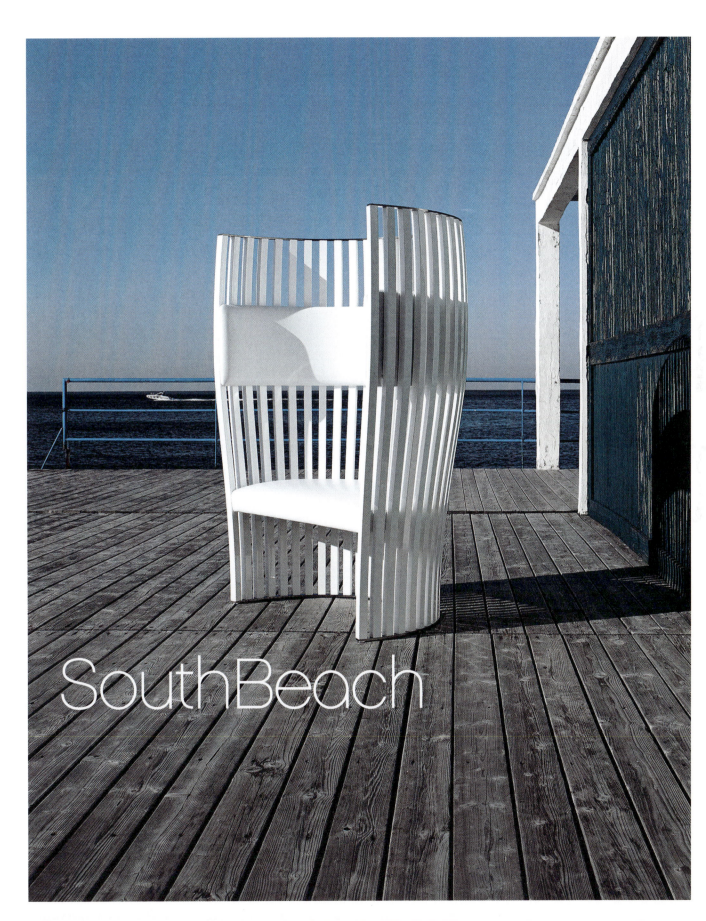

SouthBeach

Designer~
Alfredo Häberli

Manufacturer~
b.d (Barcelona Design)

Materials~
Tubular steel,
perforated steel sheet

Completed~
2005

Website~
www.bdbarcelona.com

Photography by
b.d

Derived from the same basic form and materials—legs in cold-rolled tubular steel supporting a combined seat and backrest of perforated steel sheet—The Swiss Benches are extended, elongated and adapted versions of one another. The Couple is a bench for twosomes who want some privacy. Those happier with a personal but not totally isolated space may prefer The Philosopher. For singles, Alfredo Häberli designed The Loner. Office workers who like having lunch outdoors will find The Poet's table function quite accommodating. And there is even an option for people who are tired of sitting down all day: The Banker. Adding extra value to ordinary objects, Häberli has designed a collection of benches that cater for individual needs.

The Swiss Benches

Designer~
Verónica Martínez

Manufacturer~
Gandia Blasco

Materials (prototype)~
Plexiglas,
powder-coated steel

Dimensions~
Chaise lounge:
290 x 90 cm
Chair:
160 x 90 cm
Sun bed:
200 x 50 cm
Table:
100 x 50 cm
Sun bed at floor level:
90 x 30 cm

Completed~
2007

Website~
www.veromartinez.com

Photography by
Verónica Martínez

White linear forms fabricated from Plexiglas and white powder-coated steel define Verónica Martínez's outdoor furniture collection, which draws inspiration from light reflecting off ocean waves. Rising from a flat base at various points and angles are chaise longues, chairs, tables, and sun beds consisting of slats in different lengths. The overall composition evokes a sense of movement, continuation and lightness. Suitable for both public and private spaces, the products can be made from other materials as well, such as ceramic, LG-Hi Macs, fibre-cement sheet, plastic wood, concrete, with structure in aluminium or steel.

Mare

Designer~
Herman Lijmbach

Materials~
Rotomoulded polyethylene,
milled aluminium sheet

Dimensions~
Large element:
120 cm
Small element:
50 cm

Prototype completed~
June 2007
(marketed in 2008)

E-mail~
lijmbach@gmail.com

Photography by
René van der Hulst,
Merel Kokhuis

A meandering form appearing to snake across the floor at Lift-off 2007, Herman Lijmbach's Diversity bench— a modular outdoor seating object based on biological structures—resembles a piece of coral branching out at various angles. An organic structure that can be rearranged and extended to form a multitude of configurations, the skeletal frame—with its severed ends capped in metal—provided visitors to the galleries with a place to rest and interact.

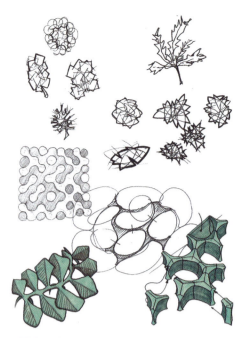

Diversity

Designer~
Livia Lauber, ECAL

Materials~
Steel tube, Batyline®

Prototype completed~
August 2005

Website~
www.livialauber.com

Photography by
Milo Keller

Slender stems rising from the ground define Livia Lauber's On the Ground collection, composed of products designed to take advantage of the spacious lawns and beaches that border public swimming areas. Mobile, as well as easy to store and maintain, Lauber's accessories make for a comfortable day of sunbathing. Her angular backrest serves as a minimalist deckchair for reading. A small elevated ashtray deters users from littering the ground, and the sunshade protects sensitive skin from the unrelenting rays of the sun.

On the Ground

Somertroon

Designer~
Gisele Somer

Materials~
Wood, plastic

Dimensions~
90 x 140 cm

Weight~
85 kg

Colours~
Standard and custom colours

Completed~
2006

Website~
www.somertroon.nl

Photography by
Gisele Somer

Inspired by vintage chairs that sheltered sunbathers a century ago, Gisele Somer created a contemporary model of the classic design, aimed at the Dutch market. The nostalgic two—seaters are made by craftsmen in Germany from sustainable timber and nontoxic plastics. Somertroon (a combination of the designer's 'seasonal' name and troon, the Dutch word for throne) is available to both private parties and commercial outfits that rent out beach chairs and parasols by the hour or day. The chairs, which come in two basic models—standard and luxury—can be customized by selecting a colour for the wickerwork and a fabric from Somer's broad range of patterns and colours. Photo—printed bisonyl cladding is ideal for branding, logos, slogans and so forth. Weighing in at 85 kg, the hefty chair is not easily blown over by the sea wind. To introduce Somertroon to the Dutch market, the designer covered a small stretch of the beach with 100 chairs: an impressive field of 'summer thrones'.

Designer~
Bless

Manufacturer~
Bless

Materials~
Plastic, canvas

Dimensions~
1.8 x 2.4 m

Completed~
2007

Website~
www.bless-service.de

Photography by
Francis Ware

Beachlife~
Products

Bless's Fat Knit Hammock, the latest addition to a collection that the German fashion and design studio calls N°28 Climate Confusion Assistance, has an inner core wrapped as snugly as an Inuit in the dead of winter. Presented in the gardens of Villa Noilles—an exhibition space in the south of France devoted to photography, design and architecture—the hammock is made from sturdy bands of canvas encased in soft black plastic. Sporting a chunkier knit than that of your average jumper, the hanging bed evokes the image of a sleek new tyre with an intriguing tread. Part of a series of products designed to be worn or used to enhance personal stability and comfort, regardless of weather and location, the hammock was displayed alongside Bless's Fat Knit Home Boots and Duvet Jacket, as well as the team's Fur and Sofa Hammocks.

Fat Knit Hammock

Designer~
Alfred van Elk

Manufacturer~
Glenn Charls

Material~
Bisazza Opus Romano glass mosaic

Completed~
2004

Website~
www.alfredvanelk.com

Photography by Alfred van Elk

Clean, light and decorative—as seen in bathrooms, spas and swimming pools the world over—mosaic has been used for centuries to finish walls and floors. Giving the material an extra dimension, designer Alfred van Elk covered the svelte form of his Pharaoh chair with Opus Romano glass mosaic tiles from Bisazza. Fit for a king and completely blanketed in 12-x-12-mm tiles, the chair can be made to order and used indoors and out. The low backrest—or armrest, depending on the user's position—gently curves like a glistening wave. Several chairs positioned back to back or side by side merge with one another to form a visual entity.

Pharaoh

Designer~
fries&zumbühl

Manufacturer~
Plastxform

Material~
Polypropylene

Dimensions~
42 x 77 cm

Weight~
2.2 kg

Completed~
2004

Website~
www.frieszumbuehl.ch

Photography by Heyer, Lozza and Rawle

Entitled Pachific—the Romansh word for 'relax and chill'—fries&zumbühl's minimal lounger invites users to lean back and do just that. (Romansh, one of the four national languages of Switzerland, is also spoken in the designers' office in Zürich.)

Resembling the seat of a deckchair that has been stiffened and removed from its frame, Pachific is lightweight and stackable. Easy to clean, the waterproof polypropylene shell fulfils all the requirements of a beach chair.

Beachlife~
Products

Pachific.minimal lounge

Designer~
Francesc Rifé

Manufacturer~
Samoa

Material~
Aluminium

Colours~
White, black,
charcoal-grey, olive-green

Completed~
2008

Websites~
www.samoadesign.com

Photography by
Gerald Kiernan

IZ is a collection of aluminium furniture created by Francesc Rifé for Samoa. Designed for outdoor living and characterized by clean lines and subtle curves, the series consists of chaise longues, dining chairs, easy chairs, tables, stools and sofas. Imitating the slatted wooden furniture long identified with an afternoon in the garden, IZ features surfaces interrupted by rows of vertical slits. Spotlighting the outdoor setting for which these pieces are intended, Rifé added special water-repellent cushions that can be left outside in all types of weather. The products are available in four colours: white, black, charcoal-grey and olive-green.

IZ

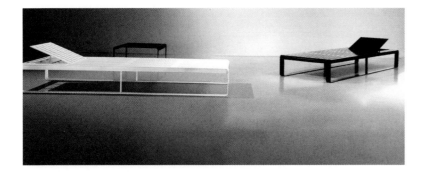

Beachlife~

Beachlife~
Architecture and Interior Design at the Seaside

Publishers~
Frame Publishers
www.framemag.com
Gestalten
www.gestalten.com

Editing~
Clare Lowther, Sarah Schultz

Introduction~
Satellietgroep
www.satellietgroep.nl

Contributing art research~
Satellietgroep

Front cover photography~
Steve Speller

Graphic design~
Matte
www.matte.nl

Copy editing~
Donna de Vries-Hermansader

Translation~
InOtherWords
(Donna de Vries-Hermansader)

Colour reproduction~
Neroc VGM, Amsterdam

Printing~
Livonia Print

International distribution~
Gestalten
www.gestalten.com
sales@gestalten.com

ISBN: 978-3-89955-302-4

© 2008 Frame Publishers, Amsterdam, 2008
© 2008 Die Gestalten Verlag GmbH & Co. KG, Berlin, 2008

All rights reserved. No part of this publication may be reproduced or transmitted in any form or by any means, electronic or mechanical, including photocopy or any storage and retrieval system, without permission in writing from the publisher.

Bibliographic information published by the Deutsche Nationalbibliothek The Deutsche Nationalbibliothek lists this publication in the Deutsche Nationalbibliografie; detailed bibiographic is available on the internet at http://dnb.d-nb.de

Printed on acid-free paper produced from chlorine-free pulp. TCF ∞
Printed in Latvia
987654321

Beachlife~